WALKS

of

the

SANTA

MONICA

MOUNTAINS

vol. 1
Central Section

FRONT COVER: Tidy Tips *(Layia platyglossa)*
                April 19, 1983

BACK COVER: Santa Ynez Canyon, Topanga State Park
                August 4, 1980.

Illustrations of Century Lake, Rock Pool, Marmot Rock,
and the pickup truck at Cold Creek, by Janet Solum

Illustrations of plants, photocopies of plants, and maps,
by the author.

* * * * * * *

Volume I, Central Section, of Wildflower Walks of the Santa
Monica Mountains is the first of a series that will cover the Santa
Monica Mountain area. Volume I encompasses Malibu Creek watershed and west to the Arroyo Sequit watershed.
    Volume II, Western Section, will include everything west of the
Arroyo Sequit watershed.
    Volume III, Eastern Section, will include Topanga watershed
and everything east.
    The data collection is an ongoing process and some of the
other walks have been written. I would estimate a book each year
would be reasonable timing for the remaining volumes.

* * * * * * *

ACKNOWLEDGEMENTS

Of the many people who helped produce this book I would like
to specially acknowledge the contributions of Carl Fisher, Jim
Kenney, Maxine McAuley, Eileen Salenik, Tim Thomas, and Betty
Weichec. Many others, some without being aware of their help,
contributed by identifying plants and suggesting areas to look.

WILDFLOWER WALKS

of the

SANTA MONICA MOUNTAINS

VOL. I

CENTRAL SECTION

by
MILT McAULEY

CANYON PUBLISHING COMPANY

ISBN 0-942568-16-8

Library of Congress Card Number 87- 72856

Published in the United States of America

Canyon Publishing Company
8561 Eatough Avenue
Canoga Park, CA 91304

DEDICATION

To those who have the foresight and commitment to set aside lands for public use; to the planners; the trail builders; the volunteers and professionals who bring their knowledge of these mountains to others — you are to be commended.

TABLE OF CONTENTS

HOW TO USE THE BOOK

"Wildflower Walks" is written so that we can go into the mountains with the reasonable expectation of seeing and identifying flowers. I have expanded the concept to include other parts of the plant besides flowers. some plants, a Bigleaf Maple for example, don't display much of a flower — it's the leaves that may be of interest — or the seedpod of the Cockle Bur — or maybe the grapes on the Wild Grape! In any event my aim is to give you an indication of what to look for and to provide a decent enough map so that you can find your own way without difficulty.

I suggest that you read the walk description before going into the field. Most of the walks will be along maintained trails but some will involve rock scrambling, crawling through chaparral or some other activity that requires boots, old clothing and a mental attitude more severe than for a stroll in the Park. The walk description will tell you what to expect — in fact, give you the type of terrain, elevation gain and distance. Some walks have been included that will take you from the beaten path. (Only one known area of "Southern Mountain Misery" exists in the Santa Monicas, and that is on a trailless Chaparral ridge. We would discover what misery is in order to view it.) We must know these things in advance and the hardships involved, particularly if one is likely to become enthusiastic about chasing down some nondescript flower while failing to realize that accompanying wives/husbands/friends would rather be somewhere else.

My intention is to offer you an opportunity to enjoy the Wildflower Walk experience without a lot of unpleasant surprises; or at least indicate when the trail gets rough or steep or brushy. Then again you may want to wade in marshes, fight the Chaparral, slide down steep slopes or cope with Poison Oak — the opportunity exists.

The write-up of the walk will usually make no mention of the commonest plants found in the Santa Monica Mountains, unless they are so plentiful or spectacular that to ignore them would be remiss. Black Mustard and Red-stem Filaree will be found on most hikes; they, along with others, will be seldom pointed out. I have tried to bring attention to any plant that makes the area special, such as the Bigleaf Maple at the base of upper Sycamore Falls, the Stream Orchids along Cold Creek, and the Chaparral Pea forest on the Conejo Plateau.

Most of these walks are on public land and are under environmental protection. We may look, measure, photograph, or sketch, but not remove or collect any plant parts.

A 10X magnifying glass conveniently hung around your neck on a length of red yarn is a great help in looking at plants. A small, 6 inch ruler is important to help identify plants if you reference book gets into measurements. Some books use the metric system, many do not. A ruler with both scales is preferred.

You may notice that most of the plant names used are common names. The book is written so that one need not be a botanist to enjoy the flowers, and those of us who care to may cross reference common names to technical names. I would like to issue another advisory: This is not a flower identification book — it is a "How to find the flowers" book. For a flower identification book I would recommend my "Wildflowers of the Santa Monica Mountains."

PLANT COMMUNITIES

Plant communities in the Santa Monica Mountains are identified by and consist of a number of unique plant combinations. Each combination defines the community, even though variations can be found in different locations. This list is described by climatic environment, and by indicator plants usually found in the community. Plant communities abutting each other often have an identifiable zone that consists of plants from both; and quite often pockets of one community may be located within another. For purposes of this book I have used the broadest definition of the communities. All naturalists are not in agreement on nomenclature and criteria, but the following list is recognizable.

They are: (1) Chaparral, (2) Southern Oak Woodland, (3) Coastal Sage Scrub, (4) Riparian Woodland, (5) Valley Grassland, (6) Vernal Moist Habitat, (7) Cactus Scrub, (8) Cliffside, (9) Coastal Strand, (10) Coastal Salt Marsh, and (11) Freshwater Marsh.

CHAPARRAL

Chaparral is the dominant community in the Santa Monica Mountains. High rocky ridges, steep slopes, and poor soil are the choice environments for chaparral. A small amount of rainfall, all of which falls during winter, is necessary for growth of the community. Fire, periodically, is required for a chaparral community to regenerate. During normal growth Manzanita, Ceanothus, Chamise and other plants deposit toxins on the soil, which action inhibits the sprouting of seeds, so that in time the forest ages and dies. Fire is required to remove the dead wood, volatize the soil toxins, and to deposit nutrients in preparation for new growth. Summer dry climates suitable for substantial chaparral forests are found in 5 areas of the world: (1) The Mediterranean, (2) The California Coast and Baja, (3) The central section of coastal Chile, (4) South Africa, and (5) Southwest Australia.

Characteristic plants of Chaparral are: Chamise, Red Shanks, Manzanita, Ceanothus, Mountain Mahogany, Toyon, Bush Poppy, Scrub Oak, Laurel Sumac, and Redberry.

SOUTHERN OAK WOODLAND

Deep soil often in sheltered areas is the normal environment of Southern oak woodlands. Smaller in area than chaparral forests, oak woodlands will often be found on north facing slopes below chaparral. Tapia Park and several areas in Southern Malibu Creek State Park are covered with oak woodlands. Some characteristic plants are: Coast Live Oak, Bay, Walnut, Canyon Sunflower, Woodfern, Bush Monkey Flower, and Poison Oak.

COASTAL SAGE SCRUB

Coastal sage scrub occupies the lower dry slopes of both coastal and inland locations. Generally with shallower root systems than chaparral, and less densely spaced, scrub plants are also much smaller. Some characteristic plants are: Buckwheat, Goldenbush, California Sagebrush, White, Purple, and Black Sage, Laurel Sumac, and Bush Sunflower.

RIPARIAN WOODLAND

Riparian is derived from the Latin word for river and we do indeed find this plant community along the banks of streams. Many streams in the Santa Monica Mountains become dry in summer, at least on the surface, but will maintain a moist zone a foot or so down. Look for Riparian Woodlands down in the canyons. Sometimes Riparian Woodland merges with Freshwater Marsh, as where Malibu Creek enters Century Lake. Plants from both communities can be found for some distance on both sides of the dividing zone, but the difference becomes distinct. Characteristic plants in a Riparian Woodland are: Big-leaf Maple, White Alder, Cottonwood, Stream Orchid, Horsetail, Sycamore, Bracken Fern, California Blackberry, Poison Oak, and Scarlet Monkey Flower.

VALLEY GRASSLAND

Originally, Valley Grassland was composed of native perennial bunch grasses, a wide variety of flowering plants and a few oaks. Because grasslands make great pastures, the earliest European settlers grazed stock on the grass, forever altering the plant composition. Introduced grasses and other plants, disruption of the

11

land by plowing, and an infrequency of fires have had an impact on the plant community. However, the change in species composition has not had a major impact in changing grasslands to some other plant community. A well-known grassland in upper LaJolla Valley is being observed with great interest because much of the native bunch grass remains. One of the walks described later takes us through Charmlee Park. Many grasslands are found here, most on gentle sloping land but some are found on steep slopes. Native characteristic plants include Mariposa Lily, Foothill Needlegrass, Purple Needlegrass, Tarweed, and Blue-eyed Grass. Introduced species include various Wild Oats, Black Mustard, Foxtail Brome-grass, Filaree, Barley, Rye, and Harding Grass.

VERNAL MOIST HABITAT

Rain will fill a pond in winter and it will dry up in the summer, or a full flowing stream will fill basins along the bank to have them go dry later. These conditions produce Vernal Moist Habitats. Some plants tolerate a changing water level — some require it. Plants that need submersion in water for germination and early growth, but a low water level before seed is set, have a competitive advantage over others in a vernal pool. Our walk at Rocky Oaks will take us to a pond that nearly always goes dry by the end of summer. Characteristic plants are Long-leaved Ammania, Waterwort, Lowland Cudweed, California Loosestrife, Woolly Heads, Alkali Mallow, Bull Clover, and White-tipped Clover.

CACTUS SCRUB

When cactus plants cover an area causing the exclusion of other plants, a unique community develops. Usually individual cactus plants are a part of coastal sage scrub or other communities but on occasion will completely dominate a few acres of hot, dry territory. Ground squirrels and rabbits with maybe a snake or two will live in the community. The squirrels and rabbits keep other plants from growing in the community and will enlarge the available land by foraging the perimeter so that the "cactus patch" can grow. The cactus plants afford protection of the rodents from hawks and coyotes. The typical plants are Pear Cactus. Neither Beavertail or Cholla cacti are known to form communities in the Santa Monica Mountains.

CLIFFSIDE

A cliff presents a difficult environment for most plants. The absence of soil, the lack of a reliable source of water, and the exposure, are more than some plants can overcome while others seem to thrive on adversity. Rock outcroppings and cliffs are found throughout the Santa Monica Mountains so we will find these unique rupicolous plants within most other plant communities.

Although some of these plants may be found elsewhere the following are usually found on cliffs or among the rocks at the base: Dudleya, Spike Moss, Golden Yarrow, Tejon Milk-aster, Shrubby Bedstraw, and California Fuchsia.

COASTAL STRAND

A narrow interrupted sand dune and green belt extends along the ocean from Santa Monica to Point Mugu. This Coastal Strand has been altered or removed from the environment by construction of the Pacific Coast Highway and other building activity. Some characteristic plants are: Sand Verbena, Silver Beachweed, Yerba Mansa, Sea Rocket, Beach Primrose, Beach Morning Glory and Dudleya. This book does not include this plant community; a subsequent volume in the series will describe beach walks.

COASTAL SALT MARSH

A salt marsh is the tidewater zone of the ocean forming a lagoon. Two are found in the Santa Monica Mountains: Mugu Lagoon and Malibu Lagoon. The plants in this habitat have adapted to survival in salt water when the tide is up. The soil in which they grow is salty. Hollow spaces in stems and leaves allow air to the roots, and salt concentration in the roots lets the plant absorb water. Glands on the leaves and stems excrete salt. Some characteristic plants are: Salt Bush, Saltwort, Pickleweed, Jaumeae, and Salt Dodder. Brass Buttons, Juncus, and Ditch Grass are characteristic of the brackish water of the marsh. This book does not include any walks along a salt marsh; a subsequent volume in this series will describe visits to Salt Marsh communities.

FRESHWATER MARSH

Standing water along the shores of lakes and ponds as well as slow-moving water in streams will support freshwater marsh land. Air tubes between leaves and roots, and air pockets as well as photosynthesizing bodies in the upper leaves of floating plants are characteristic adaptations. Cat-tail, Pond Lily, Rush, Swamp Knotweed, Water-cress, and Common Knotweed are indicators.

GENERAL INDEX
OF PLANTS

Flowering and Herbaceous

Baby Blue-eyes *(Nemophila menziesii)*	March-April
Bedstraw *(Galium spp. [3])*	March-June
Bleeding Heart *(Dicentra ochroleuca)*	May-June
Blow-wives *(Achyrachaena mollis)*	April
Blue Dicks *(Dicholostemma pulchellum)*	March-April
Blue-eyed Grass *(Sisyrinchium bellum)*	March-April
Boykinia Boykinia spp [2])	May-July
Brodiaea *(Brodiaea jolonensis)*	April-May
Buttercup, Calif. *(Ranunculus californicus)*	Feb.-March
Calabazilla *(Cucurbita foetidissima)*	June-Aug.
California Fuchsia *(Zauschneria spp. [2])*	Aug.-Nov.
California Poppy *(Eschscholzia spp. [2])*	March-May
Canchalagua *(Centaurium venustum)*	June-July
Catchfly [Indian Pink] *(Silene laciniata)*	April-June
Checkerbloom *(Sidalcea malvaeflora)*	May-June
Chia *(Salvia columbariae)*	March-April
Chinese Houses *(Collinsia heterophylla)*	April-May
Chocolate Lily *(Fritillaria biflora)*	Feb.-March
Cinquefoil *(Potentilla glandulosa)*	May-July
Clarkia *(Clarkia spp. [5])*	April-June
Clematis [Virgin's Bower] *(Clematis spp. [2])*	March-May
Cliff Aster *(Malacothrix saxatilis)*	April-Nov.
Clover *(Trifolium spp.[11])*	
Coreopsis, Annual *(Coreopsis bigelovii)*	March-May
Corethrogyne *(Corethrogyne filaginifolia)*	June-Sept.
Cream-cups *(Platystemon californicus)*	April-May
Crimson Pitcher Sage *(Salvia spathacea)*	March-May
Curly Dock *(Rumex crispus)* *	March-June
Dock *(Rumex spp [3])*	
Dodder *(Cuscuta spp. [4])*	March-June
Dudleya [Live-forever] *(Dudleya spp. [3])*	April-June
Dudleya, Chalk-leaved *(Dudleya pulverulenta)*	August
Eucrypta *(Eucrypta chrysanthemifolia)*	March-April
Evening Primrose *(Camissonia spp. [5])*	April-May
Evening Primrose, Hooker's *(Oenothera hookeri)*	May-June

Everlasting [Cudweed] *(Gnaphalium spp. [7])*	Jan.-Oct.
Fennel *(Foeniculum vulgare)* *	May-July
Fiddleneck *(Amsinckia spp. [2])*	March-May
Fiesta Flower *(Pholistoma auritum)*	March-April
Figwort *(Scrophularia californica)*	March-June
Filaree [Storksbill] *(Erodium spp. [4])* *	Feb.-May
Fire Poppy *(Papaver californicum)*	April
Fleabane *(Erigeron foliosus)*	May-June
Four O'clock *(Mirabilis laevis)*	March-June
Gilia *(Gilia spp. [2])*	April-May
Globe Lily *(Calochortus albus)*	April-May
Goldenbush (*Haplopappus spp [4]*)	
Goldenrod *(Solidago spp [2])*	Aug.-Nov.
Golden Yarrow *(Eriophyllum confertiflorum)*	April-May
Golden Stars *(Bloomeria crocea)*	April-May
Goldfields *(Lasthenia spp. [2])*	April-May
Gourd *(Cucurbita foetidissima)*	June-July
Ground Pink *(Linanthus dianthiflorus)*	April
Groundsel, Bush *(Senecio douglasii)*	April-May
Groundsel, Common *(Senecio vulgaris)* *	Jan.-May
Gumweed *(Grindelia robusta)*	April-June
Hedge Nettle, Rigid *(Stachys rigida)*	March-Aug.
Hedge Nettle *(Stachys bullata)*	March-May
Hedge Nettle, White *(Stachys albens)*	June-Aug.
Heliotrope *(Heliotropium curassavicum)*	June-Aug.
Hemlock, Poison *(Conium maculatum)* *	May-July
Horehound *(Marrubium vulgare)* *	March-May
Humboldt Lily *(Lilium Humboldtii)*	June-July
Indian Paintbrush *(Castilleja spp. [4])*	March-May
Indian Warrior *(Pedicularis densiflora)*	Feb.-April
Jewel-flower *(Streptanthus heterophyllus)*	March-April
Jimson-weed *(Datura wrightii)*	May-July
Lacepod [Fringepod] *(Thysanocarpus curvipes)*	March-May
Larkspur, Blue *(Delphinium spp. [2])*	March-May
Larkspur, Scarlet *(Delphinium cardinale)*	June-July
Leather Root *(Psoralea macrostachya)*	June-Aug.
Lomatium *(Lomatium spp. [4])*	Jan.-May
Lotus *(Lotus spp. [7])*	March-Aug.
Lupine *(Lupinus spp. [8]*	March-May
Man-root [Wild Cucumber] *(Marah macrocarpus)*	Jan.-April
Mariposa Lily,, Butterfly *(Calachortus venustus)*	May-July
Mariposa Lily, Catalina *(Calochortus catalinae)*	March-April

Mariposa Lily, Lilac *(Calachortus splendens)*	May-June
Mariposa Lily, Plummers *(Calochortus plummerae)*	June-July
Mariposa Lily, Yellow *(Calochortus clavatus)*	May
Matilija Poppy *(Romneya coulteri)* *	April-May
Microseris *(Microseris spp [4])*	
Milkmaids *(Cardamine californica)*	Feb.-April
Milkweed, Calif. *(Asclepias californica)*	March-June
Milkweed, Narrowleaf *(Asclepias fascicularis)*	May-Sept.
Miners' Lettuce *(Claytonia perfoliata)*	March-April
Monkeyflower, Bush *(Diplacus longiflorus)*	April-June
Monkeyflower, Common *(Mimulus guttatus)*	March-May
Monkeyflower, Scarlet *(Mimulus cardinalis)*	June-Aug.
Monkeyflower, Slimy *(Mimulus floribundis)*	April-Aug.
Monkeyflower, Yellow *(Mimulus brevipes)*	March-May
Morning Glory *(Calystegia macrostegia)*	Feb.-June
Mountain Dandelion *(Agoseris grandiflora)*	May-June
Mustard, Common *(Brassica campestris)* *	All year
Mustard, Black *(Brassica nigra)* *	March-July
Mustard, Tansy *(Descurainia pinnata)*	March-June
Mustard, Tower *(Arabis glabra)*	March-July
Onion, Wild *(Allium spp. [2])*	March-May
Owl's Clover *(Orthocarpus purpurascens)*	March-May
Pansy [Johnny-Jump-up] *(Viola pedunculata)*	April-May
Pea, Wild Sweet *(Lathyrus laetiflorus)*	Feb.-June
Pennyroyal *(Monardella hypoleuca)*	June-July
Penstemon, Climbing *(Keckiella cordifolia)*	May-July
Penstemon, Foothill *(Penstemon heterophyllus)*	April-June
Penstemon, Showy *(Penstemon spectabilis)*	April-May
Peony *(Paeonia californica)*	Jan.-March
Perezia *(Perezia microcephala)*	June-July
Phacelia, Branching *(Phacelia ramosissima)*	May-July
Phacelia, Caterpillar *(Phacelia cicutaria)*	March-June
Phacelia, Fern-leaf *(Phacelia distans)*	March-June
Phacelia, Large-flowered *(Phacelia grandiflora)*	April-June
Phacelia, Mountain *(Phacelia imbricata)*	April-June
Phacelia, Parry's *(Phacelia parryi)*	March-May
Phacelia, Sticky *(Phacelia viscida)*	April-June
Phacelia, Yellow-throated *(Phacelia brachyloba)*	May-June
Pimpernel *(Anagallis arvensis)* *	March-June
Pincushion, Pink *(Chaenactis artemisiaefolia)*	May-June
Pincushion, Golden *(Chaenactis glabriuscula)*	March-April
Pineapple Weed *(Matricaria matricarioides)*	Feb.-May

Popcorn Flower *(Cryptantha spp. [4])*	March-May
Popcorn Flower *(Plagiobothrys spp. [3])*	March-May
Radish, Wild *(Raphanus sativus)* *	All year
Rattleweed or Locoweed *(Astragalus spp [4])*	
Redmaids *(Calandrinia spp [2])*	Feb.-May
Rock-rose *(Helianthemum scoparium)*	Feb.-May
Sanicle *(Sanicula spp. [4])*	March-May
Saxifrage, Calif. *(Saxifraga californica)*	March-May
Scarlet Bugler *(Penstemon centranthifolius)*	April-May
Shooting Stars *(Dodecatheon clevelandii)*	Jan.-March
Skullcap *(Scutellaria tuberosa)*	March-April
Snapdragon, Rose *(Antirrhinum multiflorum)*	May-June
Snapdragon, Twining *(Antirrhinum kelloggii)*	March-April
Snapdragon, Violet *(Antirrhinum nuttallianum)*	April-May
Snapdragon, White *(Antirrhinum coulterianum)*	April-May
Soap Plant *(Chlorogalum pomeridianum)*	May-June
Sow Thistle *(Sonchus spp.)* *	All year
Stream Orchid *(Epipactis gigantea)*	May-June
Sunflower, Canyon *(Venegasia carpesioides)*	March-May
Sunflower, Bush [Shrub] *(Encelia californica)*	March-June
Sunflower, Prairie *(Helianthus annuus)* *	April-Sept.
Sunflower, Slender *(Helianthus gracilentus)*	April-Sept.
Sweet Clover *(Melilotus spp. [2])*	March-June
Tarweed *(Hemizonia spp. [2])*	April-June
Tarweed *(Madia spp. [3])*	April-June
Tauschia *(Tauschia spp [2])*	Feb.-June
Telegraph Weed *(Heterotheca grandiflora)*	June-Aug.
Thistle, Calif. *(Cirsium californicum)*	April-June
Thistle, Bull *(Cirsium vulgare)* *	June-Oct.
Thistle, Milk *(Silybum marianum)* *	May-July
Thistle, Star *Centaurea melitensis)* *	May-July
Thistle, Western *(Cirsium coulteri)*	March-June
Thistle, Yellow Star *(Centaurea spp [2])**	
Tidy Tips *(Layia platyglossa)*	March-May
Turkish Rugging*(Chorizanthe staticoides)*	April-June
Verbena *(Verbena lasiostachys)*	April-Sept.
Verbena, Beach *(Abronia spp. [2])*	April-June
Vetch *(Vicia spp. [3])*	March-May
Vinegar Weed *(Trichostema lanceolatum)*	May-June
Wallflower *(Erysimum spp. [2])*	March-May
Whispering Bells *(Emmenanthe penduliflora)*	March-May
Windmill Pink *(Silene gallica)**	Feb.-June

Woodland Star *(Lithophragma affine)*	April-May
Woolly Aster *(Corethrogyne filaginifolia)*	June-Sept.
Yarrow [White] *(Achillea borealis)*	May-June
Zygadene [Star Lily] *(Zygadenus fremontii)*	March-April

* alien (non-native) plants

This list of annuals and perennial flowering plants is not meant to be complete. Their abundance or rarity each year is related not only to habitat and seasonal weather variations, but also to the periodic occurrence of fire. Almost all of the listed plants produce an abundance of bloom the first season after fire that is way beyond the normal; some of them only bloom after a fire.

Trees

Alder, White *(Alnus rhombifolia)*
Ash *(Fraxinus spp [2])*
Cottonwood *(Populus spp [2])*
Laurel [Bay] *(Umbellularia californica)*
Maple, Bigleaf *(Acer macrophylla)*
Oak, Coast Live *(Quercus agrifolia)*
Oak, Valley *(Quercus lobata)*
Sycamore *(Platanus racemosa)*
Walnut, Calif. *(Juglans californica)*

Shrubs
RIDGES AND HIGHER SLOPES

Bricklebush *(Brickellia spp. [2])*	Sept.-Nov.
Buckwheat, Calif. *(Eriogonum fasciculatum)*	April-July
Buckwheat, Ashyleaf *(Eriogonum cinereum)*	June-Sept.
Buckwheat, Conejo *(Eriogonum crocatum)*	May-June
Buckwheat, Longstem *(Eriogonum elongatum)*	Aug.-Oct.
Bush Sunflower *(Encelia californica)*	March-June
Chaparral Pea *(Pickeringia montana)*	April-May
Ceanothus, Bigpod *(Ceanothus megacarpus)*	Feb.-April
Ceanothus, Buckbrush *(Ceanothus cuneatus)*	Feb.-April
Ceanothus, Greenbark *(Ceanothus spinosus)*	March-May
Ceanothus, Hairyleaf *(Ceanothus oliganthus)*	March-April
Ceanothus, Hoaryleaf *(Ceanothus crassifolius)*	March-April

Ceanothus, Whitethorn *(Ceanothus leucodermis)*	April-June
Chamise *(Adenostoma fasciculatum)*	May-June
Cherry, Hollyleaf *(Prunus ilicifolia)*	April-May
Coyote Brush *(Baccharis pilularia)*	Aug.-Nov.
Deerweed *(Lotus scoparius)*	March-June
Goldenbush *(Haplopappus spp. [4])*	Sept.-Oct.
Laurel Sumac *(Rhus Laurina)*	May-June
Mallow, Bush *(Malacothamnus fasciculatus)*	May-Oct.
Manzanita, Bigberry *(Arctostaphylos glauca)*	Jan.-March
Manzanita, Eastwood *(Arctostaphylos glandulosa)*	Jan.-March
Mountain Mahogany *(Cercocarpus betuloides)*	March-May
Poppy, Bush or Tree *(Dendromecon rigida)*	Feb.-May
Prickly Phlox *(Leptodactylon californicum)*	Jan.-April
Rattleweed [Locoweed] *(Astragalus spp. [5])*	March-June
Redberry *(Rhamnus crocea)*	January-April
Redberry, Hollyleaf *(Rhamnus ilicifolia)*	Feb.-April
Redshanks *(Adenostoma sparsifolium)*	August
Sage, Black *(Salvia mellifera)*	April-June
Sage, Purple *(Salvia leucophylla)*	May-July
Sage, White *(Salvia apiana)*	April-June
Sagebrush, Coastal *(Artemesia californica)*	Aug.-Oct.
Scrub Oak *(Quercus dumosa)*	March-April
Silk Tassel *(Garrya veatchii)*	Jan.-March
Squaw Bush *(Rhus trilobata)*	March-April
Sugar Bush *(Rhus ovata)*	March-May
Toyon *(Heteromeles arbutifolia)*	May-June
Woolly Blue-curls *(Trichostema lanatum)*	April-June
Yerba Santa *(Eriodictyon crassifolium)*	April-May
Yucca *(Yucca whipplei)*	May-June

STREAMSIDE

Blackberry *(Rubus ursinus)*	March-April
Cat-tail *(Typha latifolia)*	Aug.-Oct.
Mugwort *(Artemesia douglasiana)*	July-Nov.
Mulefat *(Baccharis viminea)*	Jan.-May
Nettle, Dwarf *(Urtica urens)*	Jan.-April
Willow *(Salix spp. [3])*	Jan.-March

OCEAN FACING

Coreopsis *(Coreopsis gigantea)*	March-May
Lemonadeberry *(Rhus integrifolia)*	Feb.-April
Prickly Pear *(Opuntia littoralis)*	May-June
Saltbush *(Atriplex lentiformis)*	July-Oct.

CANYONS AND LOWER SLOPES

Castor-bean *(Ricinus communis)* *	All year
Cinquefoil *(Potentilla glandulosa)*	April-June
Coffeeberry, Calif. *(Rhamnus californica)*	May-June
Currant, Chaparral *(Ribes malvaceum)*	Dec.-Feb.
Currant, Golden *(Ribes aureum)*	March-April
Elderberry *(Sambucus mexicana)*	April-Aug.
Gooseberry, Fuchsia-flowered *(Ribes speciosum)*	Jan.-March
Honeysuckle *(Lonicera subspicata)*	May-July
Lupine, Pauma *(Lupinus longiflorus)*	April-June
Nightshade, Black *(Solanum douglasii)*	All year
Nightshade, Purple *(Solanum xantii)*	Jan.-Aug.
Ocean Spray [Creambush]*(Holodiscus discolor)*	April-May
Poison Oak *(Toxicodendron diversilobum)*	Feb.-March
(old name: *Rhus diversiloba)*	
Rose, Calif. Wild *(Rosa californica)*	April-May
Snowberry *(Symphoricarpos mollis)*	April-May
Spanish Broom *(Spartium junceum)* *	April-June
Tobacco, Tree or Bush *(Nicotiana glauca)* *	All year

* Denotes alien (non-native) plant

The list of shrubs and trees for the Santa Monica Mountains is not complete. There are some rarely found plants that are not included because of space limitations. The division of shrubs according to habitat is not meant to be taken literally; there is much overlapping of species in the areas listed. Blooming months are also meant only as a guideline; there can be variations related to both the particular year's weather and the individual habitat.

The information in this index has been compiled by James P. Kenney.

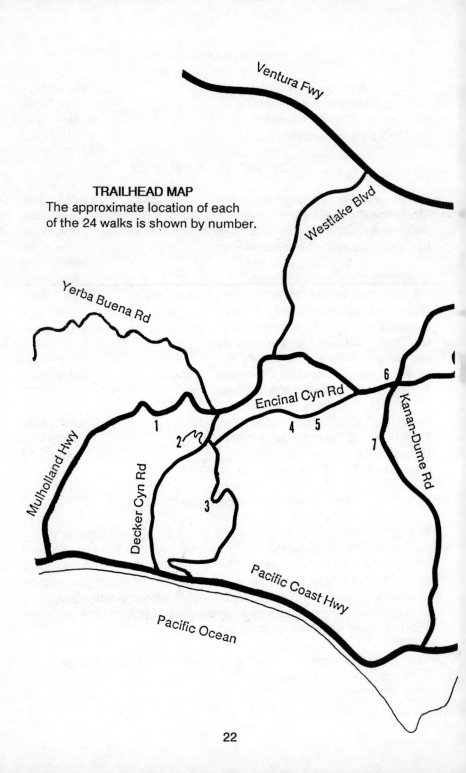

TRAILHEAD MAP
The approximate location of each
of the 24 walks is shown by number.

Ventura Fwy

Westlake Blvd

Yerba Buena Rd

Encinal Cyn Rd

Mulholland Hwy

Decker Cyn Rd

Kanan-Dume Rd

Pacific Coast Hwy

Pacific Ocean

1

2

3

4

5

6

7

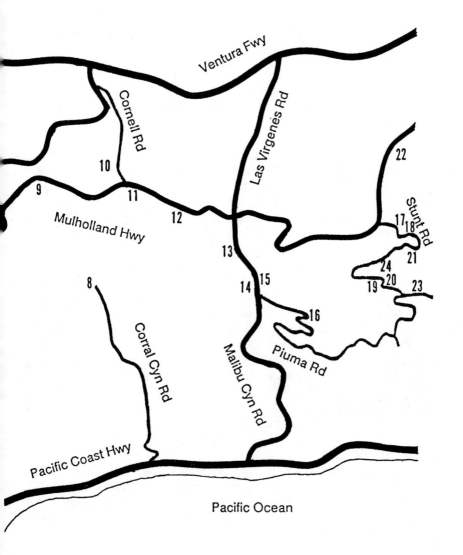

Ventura Fwy

Cornell Rd

Las Virgenes Rd

10

9

11

Mulholland Hwy

12

22

Stunt Rd

17 18

21

13

24

15

14

16

19 20 23

8

Corral Cyn Rd

Malibu Cyn Rd

Piuma Rd

Pacific Coast Hwy

Pacific Ocean

Distance:	2½ miles roundtrip
Elevation:	250' gain & loss
Terrain:	Road & trail
Trailhead:	34138 Mulholland Hwy, 6 miles from Pacific Coast Highway

AREA FEATURES

Arroyo Sequit Park is 155 acres of open meadows and steep canyons. The ranch buildings, presently consisting of the caretaker's home, a barn, picnic tables and portable restrooms are on near level areas in the center of the park. The east fork of the Arroyo Sequit is south of the building area in a steep canyon that drops down several hundred feet.

Never a part of a Spanish or Mexican land grant and used by the Chumash Indians as a hunting and food gathering area, but not as a permanent camp, Arroyo Sequit Ranch was lived on by William B. Drake following the Civil War. In 1875 he built a house that no longer exists; the present residence was built around the turn of the century.

Dick and Mabel Mason bought and moved onto the property in 1928 and used it first as a weekend retreat, then as a year-round home. In 1985 Dick Mason sold the ranch to the State of California for parkland use. It is operated by the Mountains Conservancy Foundation supported by state grant funds.

About 1/2 the area burned during a fire in October 1985. Recovery of natural growth has been spectacular and we should expect wildflower viewing to be a major attraction.

TRAIL INFORMATION

From the Pacific Coast Highway west of Leo Carrillo Beach go north on Mulholland Highway about 6 miles. The entry gate is on the right (south) side of Mulholland. The parking lot is inside the gate. The address on the mail box reads 34138. Arriving from the interior we would come west on Mulholland, 14 miles from Kanan Road.

ARROYO SEQUIT PARK

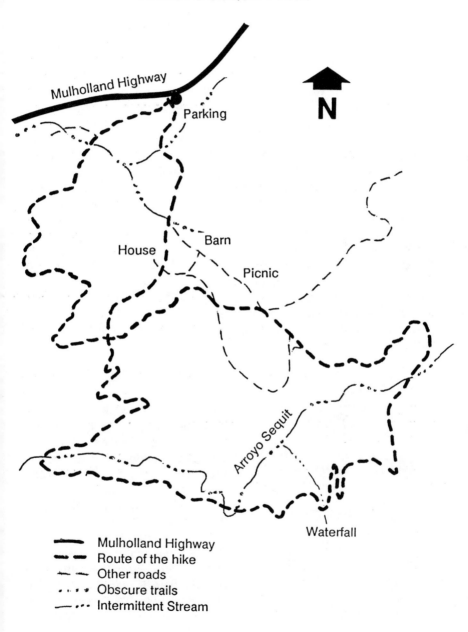

N

Mulholland Highway

Parking

House

Barn

Picnic

Arroyo Sequit

Waterfall

—— Mulholland Highway
- - - Route of the hike
—— Other roads
· · · Obscure trails
—··— Intermittent Stream

A paved road leads into the ranchhouse area and to another parking lot. 2 streams are crossed, the first one parallels Mulholland and drains the steep slopes to the north and east. Dense Poison Oak discourages a thorough botanical investigation. The second stream drains a smaller area to the east, and also is intermittent.

The trail system is laid out in such a manner that we can do some short loop walks or several variations, one of which takes us down into and out of the East Fork gorge. The trail into the gorge is south of the ranch house and makes several switchbacks as it steeply descends to the East Fork. The 1985 fire burned the entire canyon and a lot of the slopes south and east of the ranch house, so we can expect a good wildflower display for years to come. The spring of 1986 featured acres of Large-flowered Phacelia, some up to 6 feet high, Parry's Phacelia and slopes of Yellow Monkey Flower. Down in the canyon on the north facing slope, thousands of Fire Poppies were in bloom from late March through April. Eucrypta was everywhere. We can't expect this intense display to come back every year, but until the normal plant succession restores the chaparral to

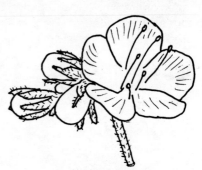

Large-flowered Phacelia

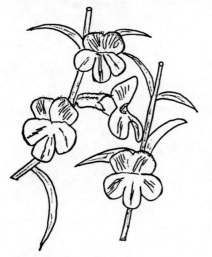

Yellow Monkey Flower

its stable condition we will continue to look for flowers that have waited years for the sunlight, nutrients and space provided by the fire. White Star Lily and Bleeding Heart are scattered along the trail out of the canyon.

An added treat in the canyon includes waterfalls. Because the streams are intermittent, the best viewing time is early in the year. The climb out of the canyon is on a well-graded trail but we will know that it is uphill.

Around the alkali marsh we look for California Loosestrife, Hyssop's Loosestrife, Water Parsnip and Marsh Fleabane. These plants are seldom seen elsewhere in the Santa Monica Mountains.

Half way between the house and the gate an intermittent stream crosses under the road. The volcanic rock typically supports plants that normally will not grow in better soil. We look for Bird's-foot Fern, Blue Larkspur, Shooting Star, California Fuchsia, Red-skinned Onion and Selaginella.

Several trails go through the meadows near the center of the Park. 50 to 75 species of flowers will be found in bloom during the spring and a lesser number later in the year, but always some. We look for a large thicket of California Roses (beginning to bloom in March and with red hips later), Blue-eyed Grass, Lupines, Owl's Clover, Catalina Lily, and many more.

Owl's Clover

Blue-eyed Grass

Wild Rose

Distance: 2 miles roundtrip
Elevation: 200' gain and loss
Terrain: Trail and easy cross-country
Trailhead: End of Decker School Road

AREA FEATURES

Nicholas Flat at 1500' elevation offers several plant communities: Grassland, Freshwater Marsh, Southern Oak Woodland, Coastal Sage Scrub, and Chaparral. Today's walk is on land that slopes from the hills northwest of the pond. Drainage of the area is by several intermittent streams discharging into the pond at its north end.

The southern part of Nicholas Flat was included in the Topanga-Malibu-Sequit land grant. The northern part of Nicholas Flat was never a part of the land grant and was homesteaded. The State of California bought the land and included it as part of Leo Carrillo State Beach. An occupied house is situated near the trailhead. No water, restrooms or other facilities exist at Nicholas Flat.

The Decker fire of 14 October 1985 burned the area, most of which was 7-year old vegetation. (A previous fire in 1978 burned more than 25,000 acres, including Nicholas Flat.) With the exception of some old Chaparral, the fire was of light to moderate intensity. I went into the area on 11/18/85 (35 days after the fire) and saw that nearly all the Coast Live Oaks had lost their leaves and that the trunks and branches were charred black. From my notes that day: "Cliff Aster and Mugwort, root sprouts 4"; Giant Rye root sprouting 8-14"; Grasses and broad leaved seedlings are sprouting in all the meadows in great numbers." We had the advantage of some rain, and also the absence of any Rye grass seeding — the Park Service policy of allowing natural regeneration only has proved highly successful. One day in March of 1986 I counted 70 different species in bloom, and must have missed many more.

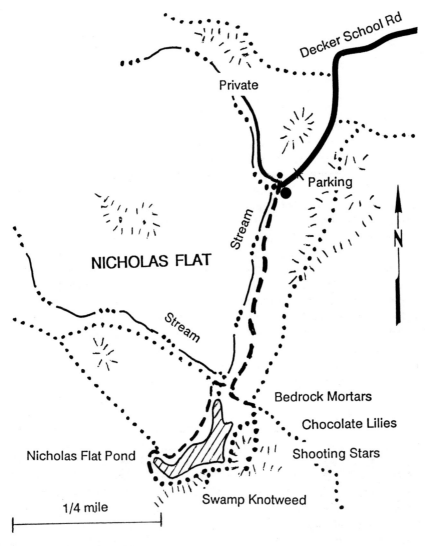

Decker School Rd

Private

Parking

N

NICHOLAS FLAT

Stream

Stream

Bedrock Mortars

Chocolate Lilies

Nicholas Flat Pond

Shooting Stars

1/4 mile

Swamp Knotweed

TRAIL INFORMATION

From the Pacific Coast Highway about 2½ miles east of the Leo Carrillo State Beach entrance go north on Decker Road. About 2½ miles north of the Pacific Coast Highway turn left onto Decker School Road. Follow the road 1½ miles to the end and park without blocking the road to the ranchhouse or the park.

We begin the walk by going around the gate, then south along an oak tree shaded dirt road. California Fuchsia starts blooming here in July and is found in sunny places on both sides of the road. A lot of Catalina Mariposa Lily, some Blue-eyed Grass and Indian Paintbrush will be found on the hillside to our left. These are spring bloomers (March-April). A beautiful stand of seedling Crimson Pitcher Sage is developing on the slope to our left — look for blooms during the 1988 season and beyond.

Soon we will come to a crossroad on the right and pass it by for now, but will return on it after circling the pond. Straight ahead for about 100 yards puts us opposite a road to the left, and of our immediate interest a large Coast Live Oak on the right — under which we will find some "Bedrock Mortars" used by the Chumash hundreds of years ago. Acorns were plentiful, and water to leach the tannin from the meal was nearby. We may want to walk down to the streambed and look for *Polygonum lapathifolium* (now called *Persicaria lapathifolia), Xanthium strumarium,* and the somewhat rare *Mimulus floribundus.*

Our next objective is the hill 200 yards southeast of the Bedrock mortars. This requires cross-country travel with some discomforts because a trail does not go there. Along the dividing line of the oaks and the sloping meadow we find Chocolate Lilies.

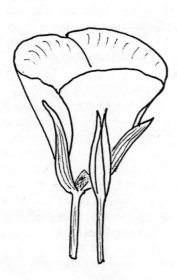

Calochórtus catalìnae
Catalina Mariposa Lily

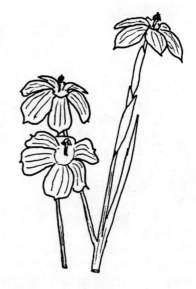

Sisyrínchium béllum
Blue-eyed Grass

Shooting Stars cover the meadow in February. On top and along the flat ridge to the south we find a wide variety of fire-following flowers. This ridge was once almost impenetrable because of the stand of Bush Mallow, but the fire has temporarily removed it. Phacelias, Eucrypta, Catalina Mariposa Lilies, Poppies, Stinging Lupine, Whispering Bells, and dozens of other species formed a solid cover in the spring of 1986, a few months after the fire. Seeds had lain dormant for many years, and sprouted after the fire. Fewer annual flowering plants were observed in 1987 — having been somewhat crowded out by Deerweed and the vigorous recovery of Bush Mallow.

Chocolate Lily

Shooting Stars

The west side of the hill — overlooking the pond — is shaded by Coast Live Oaks. Here we will find Crimson Pitcher Sage, Golden Yarrow, Roses and Bush Monkey Flower. We will want to walk around the pond, going left past the outlet. Climbing over the boulders along the south side is adventuresome and risky because of Poison Oak, but the view of Swamp Knotweed growing in the water at the base of a cliff justifies the route. Both Narrow-leaved and Broad-leaved Cat-tails grow along the pond's edge. A trail takes us from the oak grove at the south of the pond and leads to the road out.

31

Distance:	2½ miles
Elevation:	600' gain and loss
Terrain:	Dirt road and trail
Trailhead:	Encinal Canyon Road

AREA FEATURES:

Charmlee Park covers 460 acres of rolling meadowland surrounded by rocky ridges and steep mountain slopes. The major plant communities include Grassland, Coastal Sage Scrub, Southern Oak Woodlands and Chaparral. The trail system takes visitors through meadows into secluded woodlands, to ridgetops and ocean views. The land was acquired by the Los Angeles County Department of Parks and Recreation in 1968 from what was once part of the Topanga-Malibu-Sequit land grant. Charmain and Leonard Swartz were the previous owners and we believe that Charmlee was derived from the combined first names. A fire started on 14 October 1985, and burned the Park.

Facilities include drinking water, restrooms, a picnic area and a Nature Center.

TRAIL INFORMATION

From the Pacific Coast Highway west of Zuma Beach go north on Encinal Canyon Road about 4 miles to the entrance on the left (west) side. Drive in and park in one of several designated lots. The Nature Center is located on the right of the entry road near where we park. A picnic area south of the parking area is a good spot for a group to gather before starting the wildflower walk.

Bob Muns in his Checklist of the Flora of Charmlee Regional Park, has listed 216 plants. Of these, 4 are designated "rare or uncommon species." They are: Santa Susana Tarweed, Popcorn Flower, Mouse Ear Chickweed, and Blue Toadflax. Today's walk will take us to Santa Susana Tarweed. As a matter of fact we will also find many tarweeds growing among the rocks west of the parking lot.

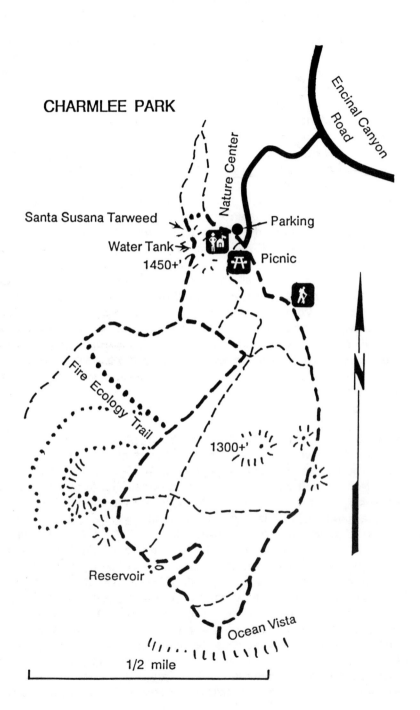

CHARMLEE PARK

Encinal Canyon Road

Nature Center

Santa Susana Tarweed

Water Tank

1450+'

Parking

Picnic

Fire Ecology Trail

1300+'

Reservoir

Ocean Vista

1/2 mile

33

We will leave the picnic area by walking on a trail to the left, initially in the shade of Coast Live Oaks. Later it goes through a succession of Chaparral, Coastal Sage Scrub and Grassland plant communities. We might take note on the progress of oak grove development here. Hundreds of oak seedlings sprouted in the spring of 1986. Many will not survive, but with a little luck the oak woodlands should prosper. This is of interest for long range planning because oak groves make good picnic areas. California Goldenrod blooms late in summer and can be found in the fringes of a woodland, usually in an arroyo where underground moisture exists. Our trail crests out on a small saddle. On the left an indistinct trail takes us a short distance to a rocky overlook point. Look for Hoary Fuchsia and Wand Chicory, both summer bloomers.

Back on the trail we come to a fork and go left, downhill. Side trails are going to show up all along this trail; we might care to investigate some or all, but basically we will continue to work our way south, joining a road that follows along the eastern edge of the meadow. When we intersect a road we angle left. We pass an oak grove and boulders — a good spot for a break or lunch. Soon we will come to a trail branching left from the road. We take the trail so as to reach "Ocean Vista," with a good view of the Pacific 1250' below and .7 mile away. Other than the view we will find Potentilla, Slender Tarweed, Woolly Aster, Ashy-leaf Buckwheat, Wand Chicory and Sawtooth Goldenbush.

The trail begins to climb as we continue west, and after 2 switchbacks crests out near some Eucalyptus trees in view of a concrete reservoir. Beyond the west end of the reservoir a trail goes south for a few hundred feet, then we come back. Redberry is found on the left side going out, as a dense clump of small leaves on spiny branches. We find both Woolly Aster and Fleabane Aster on the same trail. It is easy to misidentify the two, but look at the row(s) of bracts below the flower cluster; if the bracts (phyllaries) are shingled, it's Woolly Aster; if the bracts are long, narrow and in 1 row only, it's a Fleabane Aster.

After leaving the reservoir we want to intersect the east-west road about 1/3 mile away at the north end of the meadow. Enroute we could go northwest a few hundred yards to an oak grove on a rocky outcropping. One of many picturesque lunch spots in the park, it is also significant because Santa Susana Tarweed grows on the rock outcrop on the western edge of the woodland. To me, raspberries taste like Santa Susana Tarweed smells — rather nice. We also look for Hoary Fuchsia, Redberry and Giant Rye. Back to the meadow and, because of the many trails and roads, we have our choice. Turkey Mullein stays gray-green throughout the summer so it becomes evident when most of the meadow plants are dying back. Also this meadow is somewhat unusual in that we find a collarless California Poppy in bloom in August. Some Wild Radish is found here, often extending its blooming season well into summer. When we reach the East-West road turn left and go west, uphill.

We are again confronted with more roads than needed but because our next objective is to reach the high ridge that has the water tank, we stay on this road as it contours around the hillside. After passing an extended display of Wand Chicory on both sides, we reach an intersection with one road going downhill to the left, following a southwest ridge. (See next paragraph for an optional added area of the walk.) We turn right and have the water tank in view on the right. Immediately after passing the side road to the tank we will see a rock outcropping on the left: *Hemizonia minthornii*, Santa Susana Tarweed — the reason we came on the walk! (It blooms in July and August). Stay on the road, make a U-turn right and we will be at the Nature Center.

A Fire Ecology Trail can be added to our walk by turning left and going downhill at the intersection noted in the previous paragraph. About 1/4 mile down the road look for a trail on the left. The Fire Ecology Trail is marked by viewing posts along the way. Obtain a pamphlet at the Nature Center explaining each viewpoint.

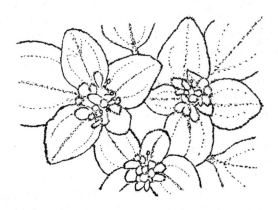

Turkey Mullein

35

4

(UPPER)

Distance:	3 miles roundtrip
Elevation:	600' loss and gain
Terrain:	Trail, boulder streambed (and 3d class rock climbing downstream of the walk)
Trailhead:	Encinal Canyon Road

AREA FEATURES

Trancas Canyon is under jurisdiction of the National Park Service and as of this writing is a pristine canyon with few signs of evident use. There are no drinking fountains, benches, tables, toilets, signs or anything else to detract from the natural splendor. The unmaintained trail survives only through use of a few hikers. This is truly a delightful spot for those who would separate themselves from civilization, and one should be prepared to "rough it" through some brush, and over some "cobbley" trail. Downstream travel beyond 1½ miles requires some rock climbing ability.

In years to come we might expect an overnight camp on the flat ground in an oak grove alongside the stream. The proposed Backbone Trail will touch the upper part of the canyon on its way from Zuma to points west so we can look for changes in the future.

The walk described here goes through a Chaparral plant community, and after a few minutes enters a Riparian Woodland for the remainder of the hike. Most of the hillside on the east of the stream is in public ownership; most of the upper canyon west of the stream is in private ownership.

TRAIL INFORMATION

From Kanan Road (County Route N9) go west on Mulholland Highway .9 mile to the junction with Encinal Canyon Road which is the left fork. Continue about 2½ miles on Encinal Canyon Road to a dirt road on the left. Park nearby, off of Encinal Canyon Road. Do not park on any part of the fireroad.

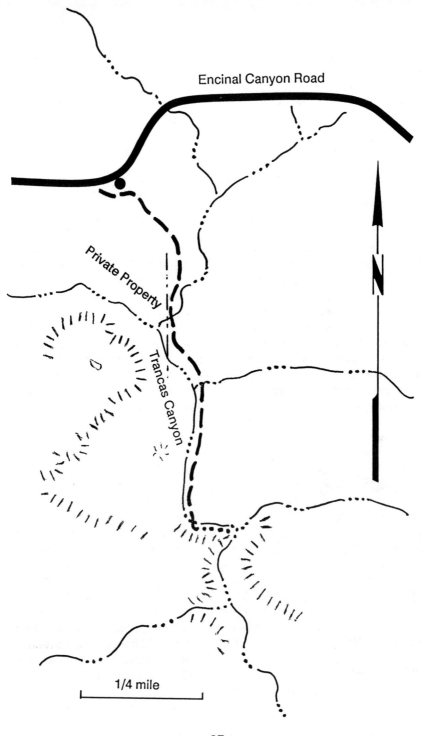

Encinal Canyon Road

Private Property

Trancas Canyon

N

1/4 mile

We hike downhill to the south on the old road, past a locked gate that we walk around, and down toward the stream that comes in on our left. We almost immediately see about 25 different flowering plants. Woolly Aster, Cliff Aster, and Wand Chicory come into bloom at mid-summer. Other Sunflower family plants blooming, or about to, in summer are M u g w o r t , S a w t o o t h Goldenbush, and Slender Tarweed. And these are before we reach the gate. Within 10 to 15 minutes the road makes a U-turn left in order to cross the stream, but we prefer to go straight ahead

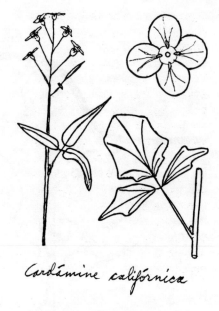

Cardámine califórnica

Milkmaids

past the Tecate Cypress, down under the Willows and across the stream, then back up the bank to the road/trail. A fence on the right at the stream is a reminder that we are close to private property on the west. It is our responsibility to stay on the trail and not enter private property.

Xánthium strumárium

Cockle Bur

Overlook points along the next couple hundred yards of trail afford a good view of the Riparian Woodland below. Some of the Sycamore trees have a trunk 30" in diameter and dominate the streambed. The trail downstream is overgrown with Bush Mallow, Coyote Brush, and Woolly Aster, Both Hoary Fuchsia and California Fuchsia are found here. We enter a level Oak Woodland in the complete shade of Coast Live Oaks. The understory of plants includes Blackberries in thick 3' high beds scattered throughout, Poison Oak, many Bush Lupines, Robust Vervain, Gooseberries and Toyon. A side stream enters from the east and is a continuation of the Oak Woodland. We will see hundreds of Milkmaids here in January. We continue downstream in a narrowing Oak Woodland until reaching the stream and a Riparian community.

Mimulus guttatus

Creek Monkey Flower

The year-round stream has cut a channel through ledges of solid sandstone. Water carved grottos and tumbling falls become common.

We will see Water Cress, Scarlet Monkey Flower, Creek Monkey Flower, Humboldt Lily, White Hedge Nettle, Broad-leaved Cat-tail, Red-skinned Onion, Cockle Bur, and Rabbitfoot Grass. In a few minutes we will come to a waterfall that presents a climbing challenge. This is the turnaround point. Beyond presents some class 3 rock climbing and maybe a dunking in the pool. A rock ridge west of the stream is sometimes used as a route. A fixed rope helps descending a cliff, and ascending on the return. Some deep pools and a cliff of solid fossil oyster shells are found farther downstream, but we don't need to know this, we've already turned around.

The walk out is all uphill but can be completed in 45 minutes, even with some stopping to take another look at the flowers.

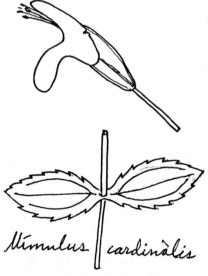

Mimulus cardinalis

Scarlet Monkey Flower

Distance:	4 miles roundtrip, or less
Elevation:	500' loss and gain
Terrain:	Trail and streambed
Trailhead:	Encinal Canyon Road

AREA FEATURES:

Upper Zuma Canyon is a rugged wilderness south of Saddle Rock. Chaparral covers most of the hillsides, Riparian Woodlands line most of the streams. and a few substantial Southern Oak Woodlands are found in protected areas. A fire burned the area in 1978, bringing about a regeneration of plant communities.

Recycling ponds are at the trailhead along Encinal Canyon Road, and some conflict in use of the area has developed. As of this writing the trail is often unusable when water is sprayed in the area and we might be required to select an alternate route into the canyon. Some of the land has not been acquired by the National Park Service and trails will not be built and maintained until such time as a route can be built on public property. Alternate routes into the canyon are available, and when the Backbone Trail is built we will have additional access. It is our responsibility to avoid crossing private property so that we can avoid a public use/land-owner conflict.

TRAIL INFORMATION

The Encinal Canyon Road Trailhead is reached by driving west of Kanan Dume Road on Mulholland Highway. Go 0.9 mile to a fork in the Road. Take the left fork — Encinal Canyon Road — and continue 1/2 mile. Room to park a couple of cars is found on the left side of the road near the recycling pools.

After parking on Encinal Canyon Road we take the left of two roads. The one on the right says "Buzzards Roost;" it is the Zuma Ridge Motorway and works up the ridge. The left road drops down along the recycling ponds, through the water spray and Poison Oak.

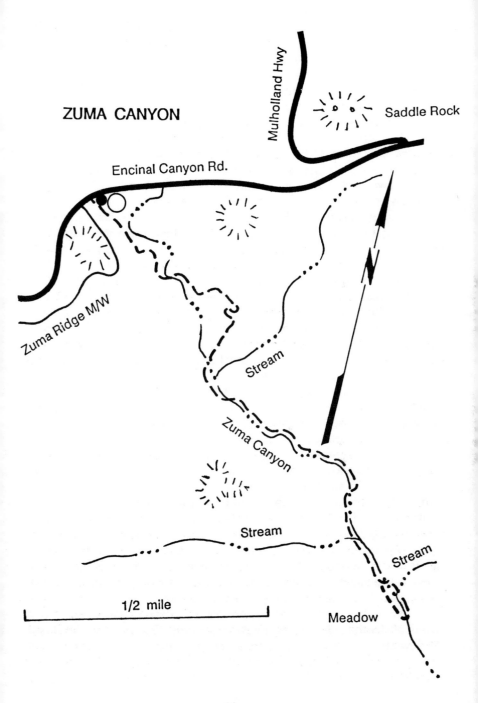

ZUMA CANYON

Mulholland Hwy

Saddle Rock

Encinal Canyon Rd.

Zuma Ridge M/W

Stream

Zuma Canyon

Stream

Stream

Meadow

1/2 mile

The road quickly becomes a trail that parallels the stream and for a time is in dense shade, but soon emerges into Chaparral that is recovering from the fire of 1978.

The top of Upper Zuma Waterfall will come into view so it's worth a sidetrip of a hundred feet or so. Cat-tails, Arroyo Willow and Fremont Cottonwood are doing well near the stream. Look for both Fuchsia species between the trail and stream.

We continue south on the trail noting that Bush Mallow and Deerweed dominate the upper part of this southwest facing slope and will for a few more years after the fire; the trail has become overgrown and is brushy in places. We make two switchbacks then steeply drop down a ridge toward the stream. Several of the uncommon Nevin's Brickellbush shrubs are near the first switchback. Look for them to bloom in the fall. The trail down the ridge is on volcanic rock, always a good place to look for Chalk Dudleya. Upper Zuma Waterfall is in view from the trail. An intermittent stream comes in from the left where the ridge meets the valley floor. We will look for Red-skinned Onion and Yellow Monkey Flower along this streambed.

After the side stream exploration we will continue to the main stream, and find that the trail forks both up and downstream—others also have tried to find the best place to cross. We will see a lot of rose bushes, California Goldenrod, Cat-tails and Willows. I like to cross the stream and fight through the willows at the same time. Sometime in the future I will come back here and find a bridge and a real trail, maybe even a sign telling me where to go, but now part of the fun is in the exploration. Once across the stream we continue left, heading southeast. Prickly Phlox on the right, Western Goldenrod on the left and a thicket of roses ahead. We cross the stream again so as to be on the left side and are in the midst of more roses. Soon we may choose to walk in the streambed, if dry, and look for Red-skinned Onions growing on the rocky banks.

At this point Zuma Creek is channelled through massive volcanic boulders, many of which have a conglomerate pattern. When the stream is flowing, we use the trail on the east bank. As the streambed comes through a small steep-walled gorge and makes a turn to the right, we find Annual Paintbrush, Tejon Milk Aster and off to the left a large Fuchsia-flowered Gooseberry. We'll see Ragweed, Onion and Selaginella before coming to a major arroyo on the left. About 100 yards into the arroyo, a cliff that in the spring could be a waterfall, puts a stop to farther exploration. We will take a look because treelike Red Shank is found here and blooms in July and August. Yellow Monkey Flower, Meadow Rue, California Fuchsia and a variety of spring blooming plants are here.

Continuing down the main stream we get out of the creek bed and onto the trail because Arizona Ash trees are getting thick along the banks. The trail is flanked with Hoary-leaved Ceanothus as we make a little climb into Chaparral. After passing some Scarlet Larkspur and California Everlasting (smells like Maple Sugar) we need to get off the trail, go through some Chamise and Woolly Blue Curls (look for Indian Warrior in the Chamise) and cross the stream onto a meadow. We will see a lot of willows at the stream crossing.

Upon reaching the meadow we will find Coffeeberry bushes on the perimeter—berries begin to ripen in September. The meadow changes with the seasons so in the spring we look for Clarkia species, Mariposa Lily, Blue Dicks, Owl's Clover, Crimson Sage, Soap Plant and Mountain Dandelion. Late summer finds Wand Buckwheat, Sticky Madia, Chaparral Honeysuckle and Woolly Aster in bloom. For the purpose of this walk, the meadow is the turnaround point, and we go back the way we came.

Wild Rose

43

Distance: I - 2 miles
Elevation: Approximately 200' gain & loss
Terrain: Trail
Trailhead: Mulholland Hwy

AREA FEATURES

Rocky Oaks Ranch was a working cattle ranch with barns, sheds and farm equipment for 30 years prior to the destruction caused by the I978 Agoura fire. The Santa Monica Mountains National Recreation Area now manages the property. Facilities include drinking water, restrooms, picnic tables, an amphitheater seating more than I00 people, and a trail system.

The Park features a woodland of Coast Live Oaks, a pond that becomes dry some years, small grasslands, areas of Coastal Sage Scrub, and chaparral covered slopes and ridges. The lowest elevation at 1300' is at the northwest corner of the property (not accessible by trail). The highest elevation at 2050' is on the southwest-northeast trending ridge that dominates the skyline northwest of the picnic area and pond.

From a wildflower enthusiast's point of view we will go to see the spring flowers throughout the area and in particular the trail that goes along the intermittent stream about 1/2 mile west of the picnic area. Of special interest to dedicated botanists a small colony of Southern Mountain Misery *(Chamaebatia australis)* grows on a chaparral ridge as a disjunct from its normal habitat to the south of us. No trail is near so we will miss seeing these plants. Summer interest will center around the pond.

The rocky peak 1/2 mile west of the picnic area is "Mitten Mountain" and 3/4 mile farther west but out of sight, is "Saddle Rock."

TRAIL INFORMATION

From the Ventura Freeway go South on Kanan Road to Mulholland Highway. Turn west (right) on Mulholland and right again into the parking lot. From the Pacific Coast Highway go north on Kanan-Dume Road to Mulholland Highway. Turn west (left) and then right into the parking lot. Parking is free.

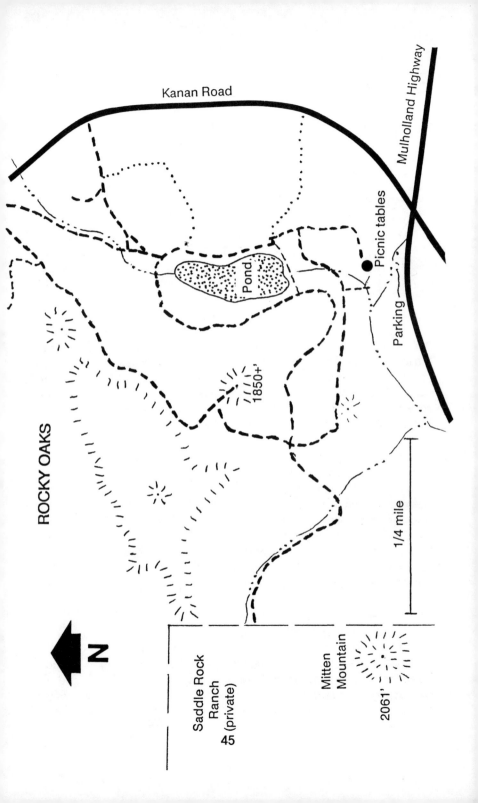

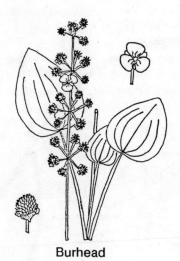

Burhead

A trail leaves the Oak Woodland at the picnic area and makes a loop around the pond. The pond should rightfully be called a vernal moist habitat because it fills up during winter rains and reduces in size during the summer, becoming completely dry on occasion. Some plants require submersion for germination and a lower water level to flower and set seed, so we need to leave the trail and get down to the water's edge to see some plants that will grow in no other habitat. Long-leaved Ammania *(Ammania coccinea)* found near the high water mark is about I foot high; has a 4-angled stem; small flowers, 4 purple petals, and opposite leaves. Look for Hyssop Loosestrife *(Lythrum hyssopifolia)* in the same general area. It has a 4-angled stem, small 6- petalled pale purple flowers, and alternate leaves. Water Plantain *(Alisma plantago-aquatica)* [*Alisma triviale*], a perennial herb having somewhat triangular stems, and Bur Head *(Echinodorus rostratus)* [E. berteroi], an annual having distinctly triangular stems, are both found growing in the water and on the bank as the pond recedes. A colony of Swamp Knotweed *(Persicaria amphibia var. emersum)* [*Polygonum amphibium var. e, P. coccineum*] grows below the high water mark on the east side of the pond. Look for *Pentachaeta lyonii* in the grasslands.

We will also have additional treats in seeing American Coots swimming in the pond and on occasion will hear the Bull Frog's "Jug-o-rum."

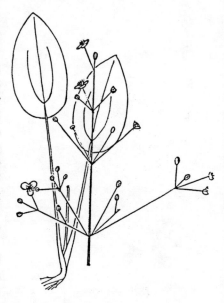

Water Plantain

The trail north of the pond will take us through both Coastal Sage Scrub and Chaparral plant communities. All of these trails are connected in such a manner that several loop options are available. Depending on the time available and the season, we might want to get on the trail that takes us west toward Mitten Mountain and follow it a few hundred yards upstream as it takes us through a woodland. We look for Speedwell and Water Cress at the stream crossing. Some California Rose is in a colony nearby. In open places along the trail look for Golden Stars, California Buttercup, Canyon Sunflower, Golden Yarrow, Blue-eyed Grass, and Bush Monkey Flower. Some Hairy-leaved Ceanothus shrubs grow in the partial shade along the trail. Late March or April will usually find them in bloom with deep blue flowers.

The trail leads to private property — The Saddle Rock Ranch — and we must turn around and come back the way we came. Maybe stop and taste a blackberry near the stream.

Buttercup

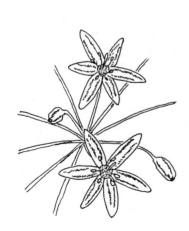

Golden Stars

Distance: 1+ miles roundtrip
Elevation: 300' loss and gain
Terrain: Trail, steep trail,
                class 2-3 rock climb
Trailhead: Kanan Road 7.8 miles
                south of Ventura Freeway

AREA FEATURES;

Newton Creek drains the steep western slope of Castro Peak, and cuts a spectacular rock walled canyon through massive sandstone. Today's walk includes three waterfalls and the canyon downstream of the culvert under Kanan Road. The canyon is National Park service property. In time this area will be part of the proposed Backbone Trail but now it is not a maintained area and has no trails or facilities.

Riparian Woodland plants are featured on this walk, and also California Barberry *(Berberis pinnata)*.

TRAIL INFORMATION

From the Ventura Freeway go south 7.8 miles on Kanan Road to a dirt parking lot on the west side of the road. A mileage marker nearby reads: 9.27 (the Ventura County line is 9.27 miles north on Kanan). The parking area can hold at least 50 cars.

A rocky road leads downhill from the western edge of the parking area through chaparral: initially Greenbark Ceanothus, Bigpod Ceanothus, and Bush Mallow, then Chamise and Laurel Sumac. Three minutes from beginning the walk and after a switchback, we turn right on a dirt road and continue downhill. Again we see trails branching right but continue ahead because the mountainside is very steep. After passing a 5' diameter boulder on the right we continue about 200 ft. before going down a trail on the right. The trail is not maintained or even built — it just grew by common use. After a steep, brushy descent we should be on a sandstone ledge, identified by growth of Seleginella and Bird's-foot Fern.

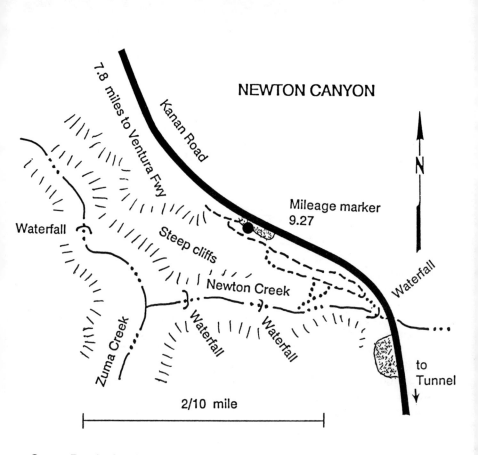

NEWTON CANYON

7.8 miles to Ventura Fwy

Kanan Road

Mileage marker 9.27

N

Waterfall

Steep cliffs

Newton Creek

Zuma Creek

Waterfall

Waterfall

Waterfall

to Tunnel

2/10 mile

Some Pectin fossils and other imprints of shellfish can be found on the ledge. About 100' downstream, a six foot cliff can be down-climbed by agile climbers. Have both hands free and someone to help because the "walk" has now changed to "climb" and "rock scramble."

Fall is a good time of year to travel the stream. The water is at its lowest, and because the shade of Sycamore and Willow trees prevents direct sunlight, many flowers will be in bloom. Look for Fuchsia along the banks, Scarlet Monkey Flower near the stream, Western Goldenrod, and Ashy-leaf Buckwheat on the sunny bank facing south.

Downstream we climb around Middle Waterfall — a 9' drop. Look for Leather Root, Cat-tail, White Hedge-nettle, and

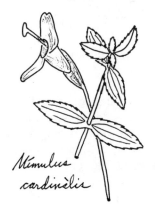

Mimulus cardinalis

Scarlet Monkey Flower

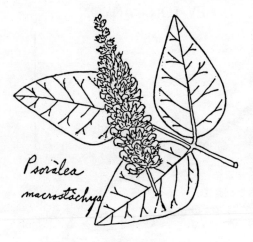

Psoralea
macrostachya

Leather Root

Veronica. The north facing slope supports Bay trees, Wood Ferns, Goldback Ferns, and some Walnut trees. After crawling under branches, along ledges and balancing on rocks, we come to the top of Lower Waterfall, a sheer drop of 50 feet. This is our turnaround point and we retrace our steps upstream. Upper Waterfall is about 100 yards beyond the point where we entered the streambed. We came on this walk to see California Barberry plants —

rarely seen in the Santa Monica Mountains — so look along the north facing canyon wall from Upper Waterfall downstream about 200 feet. A grooved sheet of calcium carbonate extends the 25 foot length of the falls. Venus Maiden-hair and moss drape down the sides.

Return by the same route we came.

Vinca
major

Periwinkle

If all we want to look at is Barberry, we can go directly to the top of Upper Waterfall without entering the lower streambed. The plants are growing in the sandstone on the north facing slope at the top of the falls. Periwinkle (Vinca major) also grows along the upper stream but is not likely to be mistaken for Barberry.

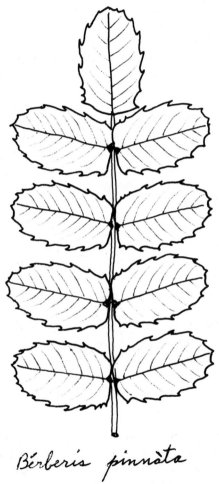

Bérberis pinnàta

California Barberry

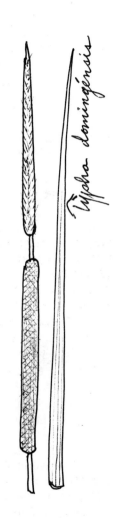

Narrow-leaved Cat-tail

8

Distance:	4 miles
Elevation:	1050' loss and gain
Terrain:	Fireroad and trail
Trailhead:	Corral Canyon Road

AREA FEATURES

Upper Solstice Canyon is National Park Service land adjacent to Malibu Creek State Park and is interconnected by trails. The Backbone Trail follows the east-west ridge on Mesa Peak Motorway and Castro Motorway.

Streamside and chaparral habitats are featured. Plants not commonly seen in other parts of the Santa Monica Mountains include: Santa Susana Tarweed, Hawkweed, Wild Brodiaea, Mountain Dandelion, Wedge-leaved Horkelia, Wright's Buckwheat, Silver Lotus, and Chaparral Pea. The entire area burned in October 1982 during the Dayton Canyon fire.

TRAIL INFORMATION

The trailhead is reached by driving west on the Pacific Coast Highway to Corral Canyon Road, a little over 2 miles west of Malibu Canyon Road. The road marker reads 50.36. Turn north and drive uphill on a paved winding road about 5½ miles. A large dirt parking area beyond the pavement will accommodate at least 50 cars.

Southeast of the parking area we see a finback of Sespe Formation sandstone. A short walk of 200 yards will take us to it, where we will find Santa Susana Tarweed plants growing out of the rock. Years ago the ridge was bulldozed, possibly to the reseeding advantage of Santa Susana Tarweed, Wand Chicory, and woolly Aster — all fall blooming and doing well.

Upon returning to the parking area after this little warm-up, we find the trail on the west side and go downhill, cross a stream-bed, go beneath a power line, and walk up to a ridge on the west. Chamise dominates this south-facing chaparral slope, but Black Sage,

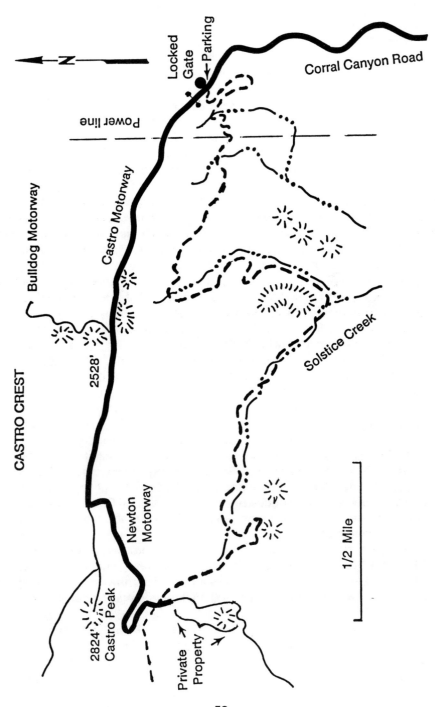

CASTRO CREST

Corral Canyon Road

Parking

Locked Gate

Power line

Castro Motorway

Bulldog Motorway

2528'

Solstice Creek

Newton Motorway

2824'
Castro Peak

Private Property

1/2 Mile

N

53

Laurel Sumac, and some Toyon are spotted throughout the hillside. The trail temporarily follows the bed of an old road then angles right as the road turns left and goes steeply downhill to a streambed. The trail contours on the right slope and turns sharply left as it crosses a stream. A 20 foot waterfall (after heavy rain only) is in view from the crossing. A few Sycamores, Mulefat, and Giant Rye line the streambed. Plummer's Mariposa Lily, Deerweed, and Rockrose grow among the Chamise on both sides of the trail.

Along the downstream segment we look for Canchalagua, Woolly Blue-curls, Scarlet Larkspur, Creek Monkey Flower, White Star Lily (thousands of lilies appeared during the spring of 1983 following the fire), and Foothill Penstemon. After reaching the west fork streambed of Solstice we angle right and go upstream. Open grassy areas produce Clarkia (4 species), Blue-eyed Grass, Golden Stars, California Golden Violet (Johnny-jump-up, Wild Pansy), Mustard evening Primrose, and California Poppy. Annual Paintbrush, Scarlet Monkey Flower, and Meadow Rue are found near the stream. Turkish Rugging, Prickly Phlox, Lomatium, and Soap Plant are found in drier areas. Crimson Pitcher Sage, Milkmaids, and Peony are found in shade. The trail follows upstream about 1 mile then turns north and climbs to a saddle on Newton Motorway.

After turning right we go uphill about 2/3 mile and intersect Castro Motorway and turn right again. Three rare, or uncommon, plant species are visible from the road. Hawkweed grows in cracks of rocks on the south side of the road; Santa Susana Tarweed and Wright's Buckwheat grow on rocky soil north of the road. We will find a Tarweed 6' in diameter on the left at the Bulldog Motorway junction. Two other seldom seen plants are plentiful along the south side of the road: Yerba Santa is found across the road from the sandstone outcrop that supports our first good sighting of Santa Susana Tarweed and Wright's Buckwheat; Chaparral Pea dominates a couple of rocky outcrops farther east along the road. Continue east to the parking lot.

Some day if we are short of time and still want to see Chaparral Pea, Santa Susana Tarweed, Hawkweed, and Yerba Santa we will leave the parking area and walk northwest on Castro Motorway. Up and back with time to look around takes 1 hour.

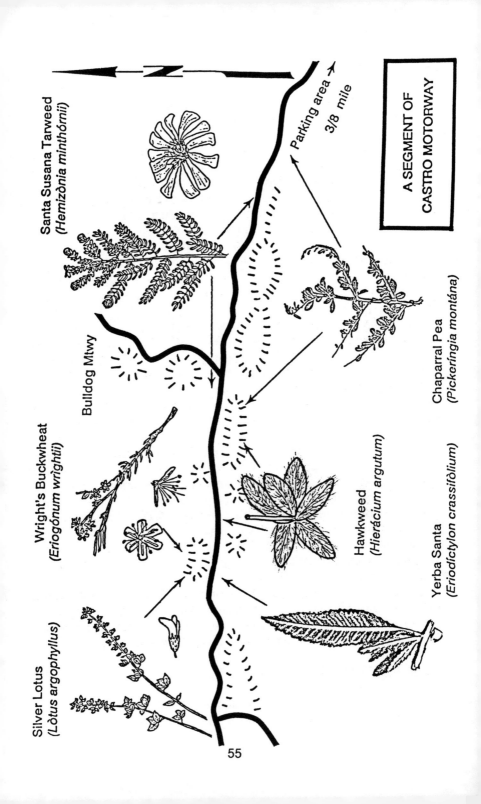

A SEGMENT OF
CASTRO MOTORWAY

Parking area →
3/8 mile

Santa Susana Tarweed
(Hemizònia minthórnii)

Bulldog Mtwy

Chaparral Pea
(Pickeringia montàna)

Wright's Buckwheat
(Eriogónum wríghtii)

Hawkweed
(Hierácium argutum)

Silver Lotus
(Lòtus argophyllus)

Yerba Santa
(Eriodíctyon crassifòlium)

55

Distance:	Main Loop Trail — 1 mile
	Mountain Trail — add 1-3/4 mile
Elevation:	Main Loop Trail — 175 ft. gain and loss
	Mountain Trail — 700 ft. total gain and loss
Terrain:	Trail, some steep and narrow
Trailhead:	Mulholland Highway and Troutdale Dr.

AREA FEATURES

The 64 acre Peter Strauss Ranch is partly on steep hillsides and also on level ground west of Triunfo Creek. A stream terrace of sand and gravel has been built as a natural result of heavy runoff during periods of rain. The stream terrace forms a large grassy area surrounded by Oak, Sycamore and introduced Eucalyptus trees. The main building, built in 1923 of local rock, is Park headquarters. A restroom is north of it. A house uphill is residence for the park ranger. An amphitheater of rock and cement was built about 1936. A swimming pool and patio were constructed in 1939. A dam across the creek resulted in Lake Enchanto, but the dam went out during a flood and nature has reclaimed the stream.

An important bit of history is preserved on the property. Northwest of the headquarters building we will find "The Land Grant Oak," a Coast Live Oak that was used as a corner marker for El Paraje de las Virgenes, a Spanish grazing concession granted to Bartolomé Miguel Ortega in 1802.

Peter Strauss Ranch was purchased by the Santa Monica Mountains Conservancy and held until 1987 when bought by the National Park Service who now manage the property. The ranch is known for holding a variety of special events, family recreation, rotating art and sculpture, and walks through wooded areas.

TRAIL INFORMATION

Peter Strauss Ranch is located at 30000 Mulholland Highway. Drive on Ventura Freeway to Kanan Road and go south 2.8 miles to

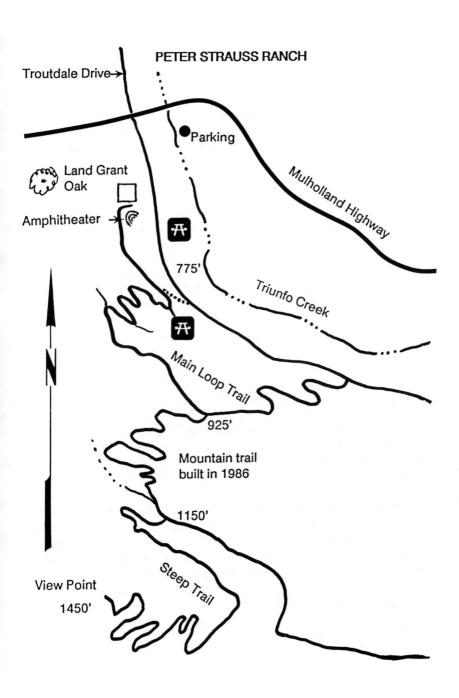

Troutdale Drive and turn left. At Mulholland Highway again turn left, cross a bridge and turn right into the parking lot. Walk back across the bridge and enter the gate into the ranch. In time, a footbridge will cross Triunfo Creek from the parking lot. Restrooms, drinking water, a play area, and picnicking facilities are available.

Two walks are available: (1) A loop trail of about 1 mile is suitable for family groups and offers a diverse plant environment; (2) A steep mountain trail branches from the loop trail and adds about 1-3/4 miles to the walk (making a total of 2-3/4 miles). The mountain trail is on a steep chaparral slope and affords great views of Triunfo Canyon.

Walk past the amphitheater and turn left onto a level trail heading south. Grasses, Pineapple Weed, and Filaree are common underfoot; a Southern Oak Woodland is to the left, and the edge of Chaparral is on the right. Look for Golden Yarrow, Woolly Aster, Telegraph Weed, Yellow Star Thistle, Phacelia, Bush Monkey Flower, and Horehound off to either side. Coyote Brush, Hollyleaf Redberry, Coffeeberry, and Buckbrush are the shrubs back from the trail. Ahead where the trail begins to rise, an unused trail blocked by a row of rocks leads left downhill. Milkmaids will bloom in February and March here. At the first switchback a spur could take us to a picnic table and swing. Instead, keep on the trail climbing past Maidenhair, Goldback and Woodferns. We will find Heart-leaved Penstemon, Fuchsia-flowered Gooseberry, Honeysuckle, and Elderberry in the gradual shift from oak woodland to chaparral.

Five more switchbacks take us on a climbing tour through Chaparral of Scrub Oak, Woolly Blue-curls, Mountain Mahogany, and Buckbrush Ceanothus. The trail levels out as it heads southeast. As we make a sharp left turn and cross a dry streambed, look for Flowering Ash, Miner's Lettuce, Man-root, Peony, Purple Nightshade, and Hairy-leaved Ceanothus.

In two more minutes we watch for the "Mountain Trail" on the right. Built in 1986 this trail is quite steep and narrow in places and at present is not recommended for an inexperienced hiker. It cannot be classified as a "walk." To the view point at 1450' elevation and back would add about 1-3/4 miles of walking. The view of Triunfo Canyon and the surrounding scenery is great. The Mountain Trail goes through a Bay Tree grove, past a number of Walnut trees, and into a high Chaparral forest dominated by Buckbrush, some plants of which come into bloom in early December.

Assuming we don't divert up the mountain, or we did and are back at the "Loop Trail," we continue east. Crimson Pitcher Sage, Poison Oak, and Bay Trees are significant plants of the oak woodland as the trail begins to lose altitude. Some steps at the switchbacks make the walking easier. More Hairy-leaved Ceanothus and Coffeeberry shrubs are seen on both sides of the trail. At a fork we turn left and complete the loop on a gentle downhill walk in deep shade. We can see both species of Ash, Sticky Cinquefoil, Heart-leaved Penstemon, and several species of ferns. Upon reaching the flat area, notice the unique children's play area. Lots of level ground and a structure that can be climbed upon should keep youngsters busy. The remains of the dam that once crossed Triunfo Creek to impound Lake Enchanto is about 50 yards off to our right. The administration building is in view and we have completed the loop.

Poison Oak   Man-root

AREA FEATURES

Paramount Ranch was a location for filming scenes for hundreds of movies, between 1921 and 1946, while the property was owned by Paramount Studios. Beginning in the early 1950's the ranch also became a site for large recreational events from square dances and hay rides to scout jamborees and rodeos. The National Park Service acquired 326 acres of the ranch in 1979 and has rebuilt the Western Town. Since then the ranch has been open to the public. The Western Town has been made available for occasional filming of commercials, television shows and movies. Hiking and equestrian trails have been built, picnic areas are available, and programs are regularly scheduled for public participation.

The plant communities of Paramount Ranch include: (1) a Riparian Woodland of willows and cat-tails along Medea Creek, (2) a Southern Oak Woodland along part of the Stream Terrace Trail and the picnic area, (3) Grasslands, and (4) Chaparral. The Dayton Canyon fire of October 1982 burned much of the area. Recovery has been natural and in a few years little evidence of the fire will remain.

TRAIL INFORMATION

Paramount Ranch is south of Agoura Hills. Drive south of Ventura Freeway on Kanan Road 3/4 mile to Cornell Road (Sideway Road) and turn left. Go 2½ miles south on Cornell to the ranch entrance on the right. Two trails are described: Stream Terrace Trail and Coyote Canyon Nature Trail. A short loop on pavement is also included.

PARAMOUNT RANCH

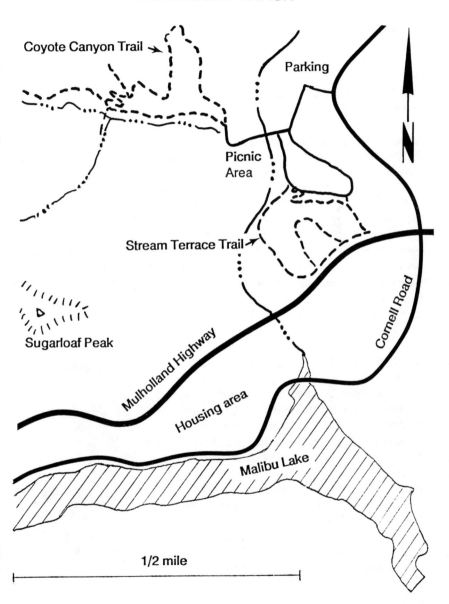

Coyote Canyon Trail

Parking

Picnic Area

Stream Terrace Trail

Sugarloaf Peak

Mulholland Highway

Cornell Road

Housing area

Malibu Lake

N

1/2 mile

STREAM TERRACE TRAIL
Distance: 3/4 mile
 Walking time: 20 minutes

Hairyleaf Ceanothus

Begin the walk south of the parking lot in the Oak Woodland on the north side of hill 860'. Go east on a well-graded path that gains altitude gradually. The trail is in the shade of the hill in rich soil and takes us through an area of a variety of plants. At the switchback to the right look for Flowering Ash on the right and Coffeeberry on the left. We will see both of these plants along the route as long as we are shade protected. We continue to climb and as we make a switchback to the left the trail enters an area of some chaparral plants. Scrub Oaks are found on both sides and Hollyleaf Redberry on the right, and more Flowering Ash. Look for Hairy-leaved Ceanothus, Buck-brush, and Greenbark Ceanothus in one area near the trail. Upon reaching a small arroyo we turn right and enter an open area of many chaparral species. Scrub Oak, Chamise, Yucca, and Buck-brush are the dominant shrubs with Western Ragweed, Verbena, Wand Buckwheat, and Woolly Aster filling in some of the spaces. We continue along the arroyo and then turn right to parallel Mulholland Highway through a sparse Chamise slope. The hill — a remnant of a stream terrace deposit laid down during pleistocene times — is characterized by gravel, silt, sand, and clay. This soil differs from the fragmental volcanic rock west of Medea Creek so we have an opportunity of comparing the two.

Buckbrush

A trail branches right making a loop to the hilltop then back down. The south facing slope is dominated by Chamise with some Scrub Oak, Buck-brush, Sawtooth Goldenbush, and spring blooming wildflowers. Toward the top look for Bush Sunflower, Deerweed, Woolly Blue-curls, California Buckwheat, Sagebrush, and on the very top, Vinegar Weed.

As we follow the Stream Terrace Trail down toward the creek, a side trip to the creek and the dredging pond area will produce interesting plants. Look for Mexican Tea, Datura, Nettles, Milk Thistle, Quail Bush, Tree Tobacco, Russian Thistle, Arizona Ash, Horseweed, Horehound, Heliotrope, Bush Mallow, and others. Good stands of Cat-tail grow in the stream and Willow, Rose, and Walnut line the banks.

STREAM TERRACE TRAIL

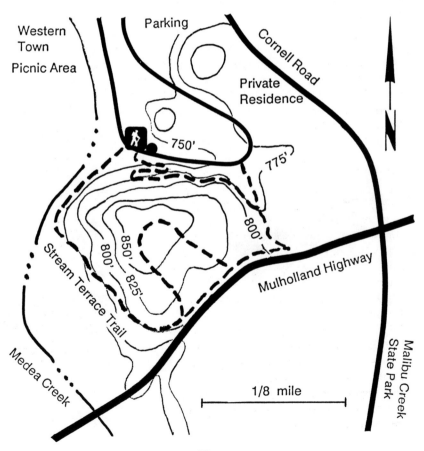

PAVED LOOP
Distance: 500 yards
Walking time: 5 to 10 minutes

This walk almost does not qualify as a "walk" because it is on pavement. The loop has some things worth while: because of relatively smooth terrain, parents with children in strollers can do this one. Also, those in wheelchairs can make this loop with some uphill work at the east end. A surprising number of wildflowers can be seen along the route. Start at the west end and go counterclockwise. On the right, about where the Stream Terrace Trail begins, look for Wild Gourd (*Calabazilla*), Goldenbush, Bush Sunflower, and Narrow-leaved Milkweed. For about 150 yards we will be going along a Southern Oak Woodland plant community dominated by Coast Live Oaks. Coffeeberry, Flowering Ash, Honeysuckle, and a variety of spring wildflowers will be the understory. At the eastern end of the pavement look for a trail on the right going up an arroyo. Several Valley Oaks are within view. At the very edge of the pavement and in cracks of the pavement, we find Gumplant, Verbena, Telegraph Weed, Woolly Aster, Wand Chicory, Western Ragweed, Turkey Mullein, Filaree, Narrow-leaved Milkweed, Wand Buckwheat, Black Mustard, Vinegar Weed, Horehound, and around the corner — Fuchsia.

Coast Live Oak

Coffeeberry

Flowering Ash

Western
Ragweed

Valley Oak

65

COYOTE CANYON NATURE TRAIL
Distance: 3/4 mile
Walking time: 25 minutes

Stop at the bulletin board west of the parking lot to check for new information and a trail guide. Continue walking west and turn right after passing the last building. Coyote Canyon will be in view west of the western town. The trail follows the north bank. A field of Mediterranean Mustard dominates the area on the left. Look for Western Ragweed, Mulefat, Madia, Sawtooth Goldenbush, and Bush Mallow along the trail — all will be in bloom through late summer. Perezia, Honeysuckle, Poison Oak, Bush Sunflower, and Cliff Aster will be seen before we have walked 200 yards. A number of Buckbrush (*Ceanothus cuneatus*) bushes dominate an area of the hillside to our right. The canyon narrows and becomes shadier. Look for Fuchsia, Peony, Purple Nightshade, and across the stream — Hoary-leaved Ceanothus. The trail makes a climbing right turn away from the streambed. We may want to make two exploratory side-trips at this point: (1) turn left and walk about 100' up a side stream to look for Flowering Ash, Small Evening Primrose, Woodfern, Crimson Pitcher Sage, Miner's Lettuce, and Chia. (2) Continue upstream on an old dirt road. Presently not maintained, this trail heads westerly along the north bank of the streambed for about 1/4 mile, then angles northwest and goes up a steep ridge. In the spring of 1983, following the fire of October 1982, Giant Phacelias covered the lower slopes in several areas. These 4' robust plants deposited thousands of seeds to await another fire. Now we will find Telegraph Weed, Sawtooth Goldenbush, California Buckwheat, Giant Rye, Mulefat, Madia, and as we start up the ridge we will be in a chaparral community of Woolly Blue-curls, Chamise, Black Sage, Bigberry Manzanita, Bush Poppy, and Buckbrush.

When we return to the Nature Trail our route is east, slightly uphill on a winding tour overlooking the Western town. Birds' Beak, Blue Dicks, Everlasting, Wild Sweet Pea, Mariposa Lily, and Soap Plant can be seen from the trail. Continue the loop and come out near a grove of introduced Eucalyptus trees. Take time to look at the Western town or cross the grassy area and relax under the trees at a picnic table.

COYOTE CANYON TRAIL

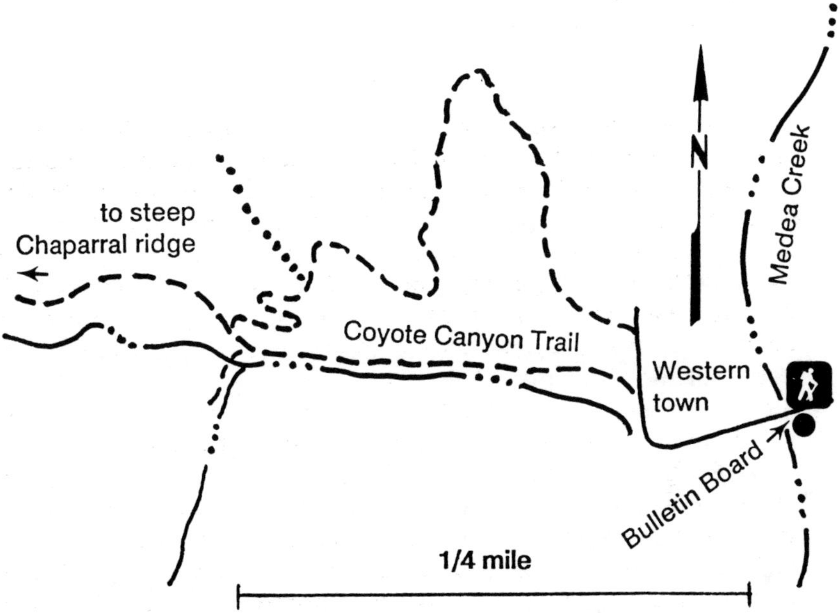

to steep
Chaparral ridge

N

Coyote Canyon Trail

Medea Creek

Western
town

Bulletin Board

1/4 mile

California Buckwheat

Distance:	3 miles roundtrip
Elevation:	400' gain and loss
Terrain:	trail
Trailhead:	Reagan ranch

AREA FEATURES:

The Reagan Meadow is a sloping Valley Grassland bounded on the south by a Southern Oak Woodland, on the east by Chaparral and on the north by Mulholland Highway. A vernal pond has been constructed at the upper end of the meadow, some introduced trees have been planted near the living area, and a heavy equipment storage area has been established. A previous owner, Ronald Reagan, used the property as a horse pasture and as a weekend retreat. Several intermittent streams cross the meadow, draining west through Udell Canyon and Cage Canyon.

The Dayton Canyon Fire of October 1982 burned the meadow and nearby hillsides. Another fire in 1985 burned parts of the area, but understandably with little vigor because of the previous fire. About the same time as the 1985 fire a bulldozer cut a swath through the chaparral from the south end of the meadow to Cistern Ridge, and along the ridge. The serious disruption of soil has had at least a short term effect on the vegetation.

TRAIL INFORMATION

Reach the trailhead by driving south of the Ventura Freeway on Kanan Road from Agoura Hills. Go 3/4 mile to Cornell Road (Sideway Road) and turn left. Park when reaching the intersection with Mulholland Highway (about 3 miles).

On the southeast corner of the intersection a gravel road leads into Malibu Creek State Park. We walk on the road, which is bounded by cultivated land on both sides. The Park Service disks the area near the road as a fire control measure, so each year we should check this out to see what new introduced plant has been blown in by the wind.

Walk south past the Park Headquarters on the trail into the meadow past the pond. We should take a close look at the plants around the pond: Narrow-leaved Milkweed, Thistle, Mustard, Cockle Bur, Radish, Ragweed, Curly Dock, and other plants one would expect to find in a grassland, but very little to indicate that the pond is a vernal moist habitat. The pond fills each winter and dries each summer and in time I expect to see Ammanias, Waterwort, Loosestrife, and others, so I shall keep looking.

Farther along the trail turn right at a fork, entering a woodland of Coast Live Oaks. In a couple of minutes another trail fork comes into view on the right. Our walk up this trail is along an intermittent stream and steep in some places. Growing in the shade are found Honeysuckle, Currant, Bush Monkey flower, Coffeeberry, Crimson Pitcher Sage, Snowberry, Mountain Phacelia, Goldback Fern, Woodland Star and many other spring flowering plants. After 200 yards uphill on this shady trail we will reach another trail (the Summit Trail) coming at a right angle to the one we are on. A right turn takes us uphill and after passing through a substantial Greenbark Ceanothus forest the trail goes into a chaparral plant community of Deerweed, Buckwheat, Woolly Blue Curls, and Sage. A water tank, then an overlook of Malibu Lake are other scenic items of interest.

At the overlook we'll turn around and go back on the same trail until reaching the fork, then straight ahead. The trail takes us through a couple of Chaparral forests and just before entering an Oak woodland, notice an elfin forest of Buckbrush and Greenbark Ceanothus. Ceanothus is a dominant shrub in many chaparral plant communities, and is a valuable ecological asset because of its ability to stabilize steep slopes. Continuing downhill through the woodland we will see Miner's lettuce in bloom from February through April, and at the edge of the meadow look for Golden Violets (Johnny-jump-up). The trail crosses Udell Creek, but because it is an intermittent stream, a few Sycamores are about all of the riparian plant community we are likely to see.

A short side trip down Udell Gorge will give us a look at Coastal Wood Fern, Coffee Fern, Maidenhair Fern, Dudleya, and Peony — all evident during winter. This area is a natural preserve and is a particular area singled out for protection. We need to use care in climbing in to the gorge, not only for our safety, but also to avoid any damage to the environment.

After crossing Udell Creek, the trail forks. We take the right fork and stay on the northeast facing slope of the ridge, initially in an Oak Woodland, then in Chaparral, until reaching the ridge overlooking Malibu Creek and Century Lake. A left turn takes us into the southeast end of Reagan Meadow where we find Vinegar Weed, Turkey Mullein, Grindelia, and Wand Chicory. From there a short walk to the head of the Cage Canyon Trail will bring us to a small field of both Brown and White Microseris, Goldfields, Blow Wives, Owl's Clover, Cream Cups, Red Maids, and Linanthus.

The return to the trailhead is northwest on a trail that follows the lowest part of the meadow. Look for a bedrock mortar in a grove of oaks. Chumash Indians were living here in 1769 when Portolá, with a group of 65 men, invaded California. Acorns made up about 50% of the diet, so oak groves were very important.

A clump of large introduced cactuses has been planted along the trail near where Udell Creek crosses. Wild Rose and Golden Currant bushes are nearby. The roses bloom from late spring into summer with a few blossoms at any time of year. Golden Currant blooms from February through April. A small patch of Haplopappus is found on the left side of the trail (see illustration on page 70). This plant blooms from mid fall to early winter. Continue along the trail.

Golden Currant

Distance:	3 miles roundtrip
Elevation:	550' loss and gain
Terrain:	Trail and Fireroad
Trailhead:	Mulholland Highway

AREA FEATURES

The upper part of the trail is on a chaparral ridge disturbed in recent years by a fire in October 1982, and a bulldozer in October 1985. Prior to the 1982 fire, Chamise, Bush Mallow, Black Sage, and Purple Sage dominated the ridge. The rootcrowns survived the fire and in mid-summer 1984 the Chamise was 3 - 4 feet high and the Bush Mallow was 6 - 8 feet high, again dominating the ridge. During the 1985 bulldozing disturbance (in control of a fire) the rootcrowns were uprooted with a result that other plants outperformed the traditional recovery cycle.

Century Lake provides an environment for a freshwater marsh plant community. Several southern oak woodlands are found along the route; and a grassland will give us a variety of plant communities to investigate.

TRIAL INFORMATION

Reach the trailhead by driving 1.2 miles east of Cornell Road on Mulholland Highway and park on the south side of the road. Room for about 10 cars is available. A narrow trail goes up a ridge to the southeast and turns right at a closed concrete cistern. We see our first surprise near the cistern — Matilija Poppies. This colony of poppies has survived several fires by sending up vigorous plants from the hardy roots, following the burning. A nearby pinetree did not survive the 1982 fire but dropped seeds and one seedling sprouted and grew for two years then died. Pines rarely reproduce in the Santa Monicas because their need for water exceeds the amount of rainfall.

Cistern Trail follows south on the ridge, then down a steep path that turns north as it drops down to a saddle. The bulldozed area on the ridge has recovered with Stinky Gilia, Cliff Aster,

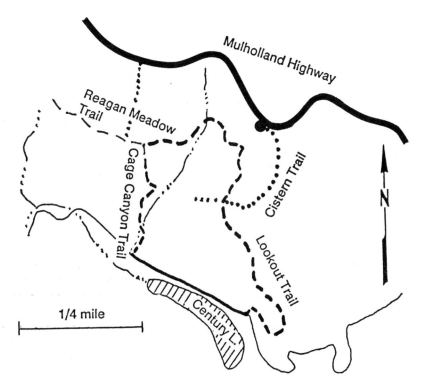

Sawtooth Goldenbush, Mustard, Perezia, Slender Tarweed, White Snapdragon, Lupines, Phacelia, grasses and of course some Bush Mallow, Chamise, and Woolly Blue Curls from roots. Along the steep north facing slope the trail is in shade of Coast Live Oaks and an abrupt change of flowering plants occurs. Look for Bush Monkey Flower, Chaparral Honeysuckle, Greenbark Ceanothus, Hollyleaf Redberry, Poison Oak, and Coffeeberry.

At the trail junction we turn left and descend on Lookout Trail. If we make this walk in March we may want to look at a field of

Pinetree Seedling

73

Annual Coreopsis found by crossing Lookout Trail, then continue to the end of the ridge. Look left down the steep slope to see a few hundred blossoms. Or go right for a look down a steep trailless incline covered with brush.

In April 1985, 2½ years after the fire, we still found many Wind Poppies on this east facing slope about half way down. Wind Poppies are seldom seen in the Santa Monica Mountains, usually after a fire and as far as I know, only in the Malibu watershed.

Annual Coreopsis

When we return along the ridge and start down Lookout Trail, views of Malibu Canyon, Century Lake, and Goat Buttes come into view. Also look for Vinegar Weed (an annual growing in full sun on dry soil), Bird's Beak, Indian Milkweed, Turkey Mullein, and White Sage.

Upon reaching Century Road we go to the lake and look for trails through the willows. Yellow Pond-lily, or Wokas, "rafts" float on the lake. Cat-tails stand in the water at the shore-line and the five-petalled Yellow Water-weed can be found in damp soil and in the water. Across the lake along the "Forest Trail" we can see some Coast Redwood trees, planted about the turn of the century.

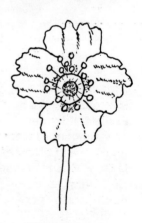

Wind Poppy

A portable restroom is currently available on Century Road, and a faucet with drinking water, at the lake. Explore on your own and maybe have lunch at a picnic table under the Arizona Ash trees at the southeast end of the lake. About 1/2 mile northwest along Century Road, a trail on the right goes north, uphill, along Cage Canyon. The trail is steep and winding but in the shade of Oaks and Sycamores. Look for Rose Snapdragon, Stephanomeria, Chalk

Dudleya, Golden Yarrow, and oak woodland plants. Cream Cups and Goldfields grow on both sides of the trail as it joins the Reagan Meadow Trail.

A right turn takes us on a tour past White Sage, Wild Rose as we cross the upper part of Cage Creek bed, and Scarlet Bugler on our right before entering an oak woodland. The trail goes through a Chaparral forest on its climb to the saddle. A left turn takes us up the steep Cistern trail and back to our cars.

Century
Lake

Distance:	4 miles
Elevation:	300' gain and loss
Terrain:	Fireroad and trail
Trailhead:	Main entrance on Las Virgenes Road

AREA FEATURES

Malibu Creek is the only antecedent stream in the Santa Monica Mountains — none of the others cut completely through the mountains. This gives us a diverse floral community because seeds from plants growing in the Simi Hills and other areas receive wide distribution downstream. Native American Indians lived along Malibu Creek as long ago as 7000 years. Talopop was situated near what is now the Park entrance and was one of the last southern villages to survive the Spanish invasion of California. Bartolomé Miguel Ortega ranched the area early in the 1800's and in 1802 was given a land grant a few miles west. In the last half of the 1800's nearly all of the basin was homesteaded. About 1900 a country club was established in the central part of what is now Malibu Creek State Park. The property was later sold to 20th Century Fox, then to the State of California. This succession of ownership during the last 200 years has modified the vegetation considerably by the introduction of plants not native to the area. We may see Filaree and grasses that were introduced early when cattle and horses first grazed the land. Garden escapes were common during the home-stead era, alien trees were planted about the turn of the century, and reseedings after fires have resulted in plant introduction. Even in recent times randomly sown flower seeds result in alien "flower gardens."

TRAIL INFORMATION

Enter the main gate to Malibu Creek State Park from Las Virgenes Road, 2/10 of a mile south of Mulholland Highway. A parking fee is required. Restrooms, drinking water, and picnic tables are available.

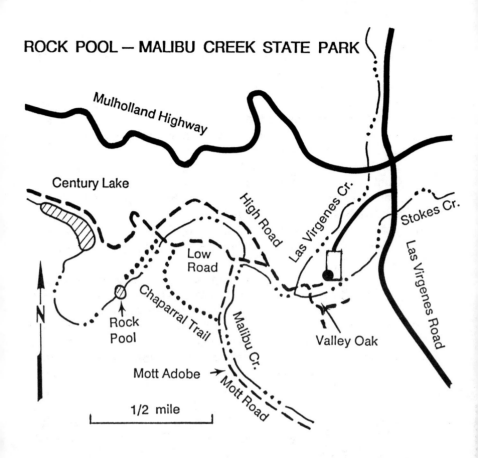

ROCK POOL — MALIBU CREEK STATE PARK

Mulholland Highway

Century Lake

High Road

Las Virgenes Cr.

Stokes Cr.

Las Virgenes Road

Low Road

Chaparral Trail

Rock Pool

N

Malibu Cr.

Valley Oak

Mott Adobe

Mott Road

1/2 mile

Begin the walk with a short side trip on the road south to a large Valley Oak tree about 300 yards from the parking lot. One day in July 1986 a newspaper article focused on the plight of Valley Oaks in general, quoting various people and organizations who proposed that something should be done to preserve the oaks. This particular oak is the largest, most magnificent Valley Oak in my knowledge so I went that day to have a look. Under the tree were dozens of squirrel burrows indicating their preference for the tree as an environment. Somewhat astonishing to me, however, were the seedling oaks growing within the trees' dripline. I counted 614 — the tallest was 23". None of these seedlings will be able to compete for water, food, sun, and space with the parent tree, but when the tree falls in a future century, one of that year's new crop will be ready as a replacement. Ground squirrels probably can't remember where they've buried all the acorns.

We will see other Valley Oaks on this walk but this is the one we photograph. We can also foresee that the oaks are alive and well — it is up to us to give them their space.

Return toward the parking lot, and after crossing the bridge over Stokes Creek turn west and cross the bridge over Las Virgenes Creek. Some 15' high Coffeeberry bushes are on the right before reaching the creek. At present the stream runs clear all year and lucky fishermen catch a fish on occasion. Watercress is seen in the shade of the willows.

Continue along the road and after a slight rise and a right turn, notice Fremont Cottonwoods near the streambed to the left. Sweet Fennel, a garden escape, lines both sides of the road. The smell of licorice or anise is distinctive. After the road starts a gentle downhill grade look for gourd vines. This plant has several names: Coyote Melon, Calabazilla, and Stinking Gourd. The softball sized gourds are fully developed by fall.

At the intersection we may follow the "High Road" on the right or the "Low Road" on the left; both meet again by the bridge near the Visitors' Center. The trail to Rock Pool follows the north bank of Malibu Creek several hundred yards before ending at the pool. Large rocks in the shade of arching Sycamore trees provide a scenic

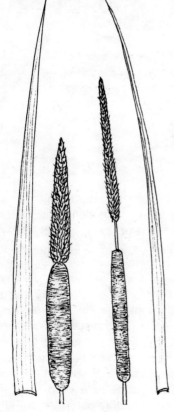

Cat-tails

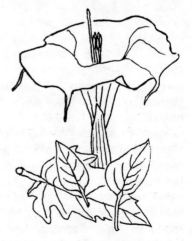

Datura

78

Rock Pool

rest stop. Look for cat-tails along all streams in the Park. Two species of Cat-tail are found: Broad-leaved and Narrow-leaved. The staminate section of the Narrow-leaved is above and separated from the pistillate section by a 3/4 inch interval. The Broad-leaved has no interval.

We turn around at the pool, cross the bridge and find the Chaparral Trail to the left and behind the Visitor's Center. The Chaparral Trail is very steep, usually brushy, and a 250' elevation gain. You may elect to stay on the "Low Road" and walk on level ground. Matilija Poppies line the lower part of the Chaparral Trail. These poppies are not native to the Santa Monica Mountains but are reported to have been introduced years ago from native stock in mountains near Santa Barbara. Good views of Rock Pool and the Gorge give us an excuse to rest

Matilija Poppy

Yellow-throated Phacelia

on the way up, and a rest stop at the top allows us a panorama of Malibu Canyon. Following the 1982 fire, the ridge immediately west of the trail's crest supported a colony of Yellow-throated Phacelias (*Phacelia brachyloba*). A few plants came up again in 1984 but have not been seen since. Dormant seeds are waiting for the next fire. Be there about 15 May.

Continue down the steep trail, brushing against a lot of White Sage and you will always remember the piquant odor of sage.

At the bottom of the trail where it joins Mott Road, a well-known magnificent colony of Indian Milkweed (*Asclepias eriocarpa*) was bull-dozed into oblivion in 1987 when the new sewage line was installed alongside the road. We should continue to look for this native plant because some seeds may have survived.

Arizona Ash

If we were to continue down Mott Road to the right we would expect to see some Datura plants. The spectacular display has gone the way of the Milkweed, but some remain. Datura figured prominently in a Chumash boy's initiation into manhood. A less than lethal dose would allow him a glimpse into the future and temporarily grant him supernatural power. Don't handle the plant — especially before eating lunch — without thoroughly cleaning your hands.

Beyond the Mott Adobe and near the stream are Black Cottonwoods and Arizona Ash. The fence ends Park property and begins Salvation Army property. This is our turnaround point.

Return by going upstream on Mott Road and turn right at the first intersection, cross Malibu Creek to return the way you came.

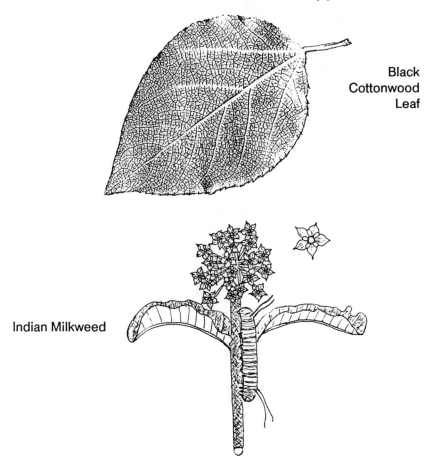

Black
Cottonwood
Leaf

Indian Milkweed

Distance:	2½ miles roundtrip
Elevation:	400' gain and loss
Terrain:	Trail
Trailhead:	Tapia Park

AREA FEATURES

The 94 acre Tapia Park is a wooded area bounded by Malibu Creek on the south and hills to the north. Facilities include picnic tables, water, restrooms, and trails throughout the Park. Plant communities featured are Southern Oak Woodland, Riparian Woodland, Coastal Sage Scrub and Chaparral. The walk as described takes us through oak woodlands and chaparral.

TRAIL INFORMATION

Tapia Park is on the west side of Las Virgenes Road (Malibu Creek Road) 4.8 miles south of Ventura Freeway, or 4.6 miles north of Pacific Coast Highway. A parking lot near the entrance will hold about 40 cars, and other areas throughout the Park are suitable for parking.

The trailhead is by the road in the northwest corner of the Park near two log segments along the road. In time the log segments will rot and not be usable as a marker, but as this is a part of the Backbone Trail a sign will be placed in a few years. An easy walk from the parking lot to the trailhead follows the road north about 200 yards in the shade of Box Elder and Oak Trees. Turn left and go west through a picnic area on a road that takes us to the trailhead.

The trail begins by going north at the lower end of a meadow, crosses an intermittent stream and almost immediately enters an Oak Woodland. Almost immediately we will see an 8' Polygala bush left of the trail at the point where a trail comes in from the west. Watch for another trail on the left that goes uphill through Chaparral. After one switchback the trail takes us through a dense stand of Hoary-leaved Ceanothus. Along the trail we look for Woolly Blue-curls, Yellow Monkey Flower, Golden Yarrow, Mustard

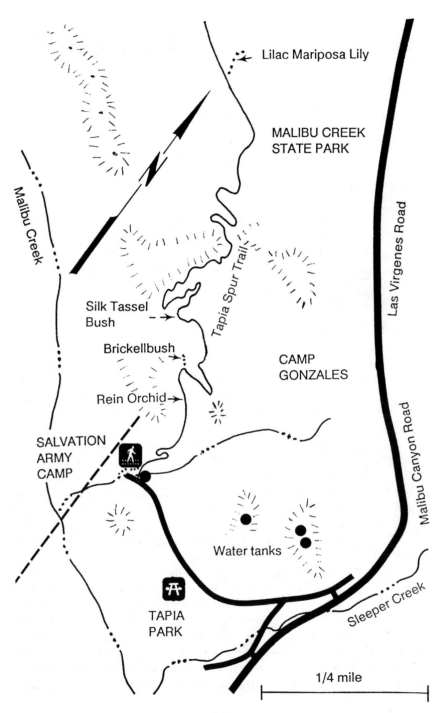

Lilac Mariposa Lily

MALIBU CREEK
STATE PARK

Malibu Creek

Tapia Spur Trail

Silk Tassel
Bush

Brickellbush

Rein Orchid

CAMP
GONZALES

SALVATION
ARMY
CAMP

Las Virgenes Road

Malibu Canyon Road

Water tanks

Sleeper Creek

TAPIA
PARK

1/4 mile

83

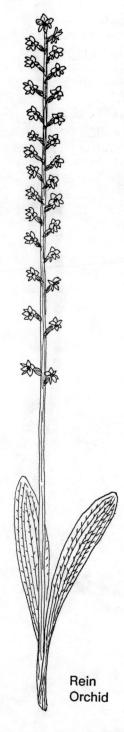

Rein
Orchid

Evening Primrose, Yellow Star Thistle, Deerweed, White Pincushion, and more.

Look carefully along the trail to the left about 10 to 15 minutes out. Several Rein Orchids grow in openings in the Chaparral. The rarity of Rein Orchids makes this walk special, so try not to miss them. We are still in a forest of Hoary-leaved Ceanothus and will see many more. This tough, leather-leaved shrub usually grows at higher elevations but is thriving here. The trail makes a sharp right turn and goes downhill through a small arroyo before climbing again. At this point if we turn left and rock-climb 100' up the arroyo and go around a pinkish volcanic boulder we will find Nevin's Brickellbush, Birdsfoot Fern, and Seleginella in one area. Back on the trail we see several White Sage bushes. After making a sharp switchback on a ridge the trail goes through a forest of Mountain Mahogany mixed with Greenbark Ceanothus, Holly-leaf Redberry, Sugar Bush, and Bush Poppy. We are given a 200 yard respite as the trail levels out in shade. Look for Silk-tassel Bush, a plant usually found at higher altitudes.

The trail soon enters the area burned in the Dayton Canyon fire of 9 October 1982. We have an opportunity to watch Chaparral recover from ashes to the present. Many seeds survived the fire and combined with growth from roots that also survived, a succession of annual and perennial plants is restoring the area to dense vegetation.

Continued climbing north along the trail takes us to the saddle where we can look north into Malibu Creek State Park and a large Grassland bordered by oaks. A short walk down the trail will take us to a picnic area and the turnaround point. Here we will find restrooms, drinking water, and picnic tables in an oak woodland. Independent exploration 200 to 300 yards north along a low ridge right of the trail would find us looking for Lilac Mariposa Lilies, an uncommon plant in the Santa Monica Mountains.

The return trip gives us a chance to see those plants that were missed. For me, uphill gives a better view of flowers along the trail because as I look ahead I see everything at eye level. Going up the north facing slope allows good opportunities to see Goldback Fern, Clarkia, Madia, and Popcorn Flower. For a few more years this trail should support Bush Poppies. Think "watermelon" before smelling the blossoms and see if you are convinced. Some other day think "cucumber" to see if your power of suggestion is strong.

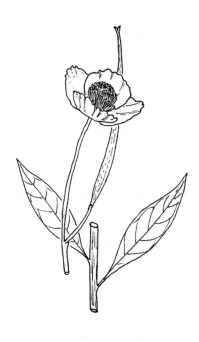

Bush Poppy

Silk-tassel Bush

Distance:	1/2 mile
Elevation:	125' gain and loss
Terrain:	Trail
Trailhead:	Las Virgenes Road

AREA FEATURES

The Forestry Nursery, Malibu Unit of the Los Angeles County Fire Department Forestry Division, was established in 1956 to raise trees for reforestation and erosion control. The Nature Trail was designed and constructed in the late 1960's and early 1970's, under the supervision of County Foresters Raymond Utterback and Carl Fisher. The labor was provided by the Fire Fighters, inmates and court wards of the local detention camps. The trail was laid out to enhance the outdoor learning experiences of thousands of people of all ages who come every year to explore and study the wonders, large and small, of this unique Santa Monica Mountain environment.

The nursery features a small nature museum, a panel display of Native American culture, and another panel of wildflower photographs. Facilities include an outdoor theater, restrooms, picnic tables, and drinking water. Hours of use are weekdays, 8 a.m. to 4:30 p.m.

A function of the nursery is to raise trees and to experiment with the growing of low-fuel-volume plants. We will have an opportunity to see this program.

A major feature of the nursery is the educational program offered to school children. Groups come on a regularly scheduled basis for a learning experience combined with an outing.

TRAIL INFORMATION

On Malibu Creek/Las Virgenes Road opposite Tapia Park we turn east onto the entry road to the Forestry Nursery. The address is 942 N. Las Virgenes Road.

We will follow the "Nature Trail," beginning near the main building. A guide booklet is available for use and tells us the features that can be seen at each of the numbered stations.

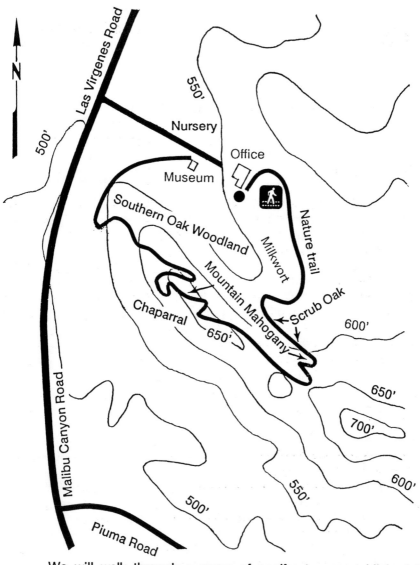

We will walk through a grove of conifer trees established in 1966. These are introduced species and are identified by name on plates near each tree. These and the other introduced trees are being observed so their ability to adapt to local conditions will be known.

The hill ahead to our right supports a Chaparral forest on the upper slopes. Prepare for a few steep places and some switchbacks as we gain altitude.

Immediately before starting the uphill climb, look to the right and see a number of 3 to 4 feet high shrubs with slender green stems and small alternate leaves. Milkwort ((*Polygala cornuta var. fishiae*) blooms sparingly in early summer. It is not known in much of California, as the Santa Monica Mountains is its northern limit. This particular hillside supports a Southern Oak Woodland — the desired environment for Milkwort — so we will see several more large stands. Look around for Coffeeberry, Hollyleaf Redberry, Poison Oak, Sugar Bush, and Honeysuckle.

Higher on the hill the trail takes us through a Scrub Oak forest. The Scrub Oaks and the other chaparral plants burned in the 1970 fire, so most of what we see now is the regrowth from rootcrown sprouting. When we walk beyond the Scrub Oaks, Mountain Mahogany, a few Fuchsia-flowered Gooseberries, Yucca, and Chamise form the chaparral community. At the ridge a switchback to our right takes us along the crest. The dominant plant on the ridge is Chamise, mixed

Scrub Oak

with Mountain Mahogany and Hoary-leaved Ceanothus with an occasional Yucca and Bush Poppy. Bobcat tracks are often found along the eastern part of the trail. Continuing northwest on the ridge, the trail dips down to a saddle and we find some Hollyleaf Cherry, Sugar Bush and California Buckwheat.

The highest point of the walk, "Little Whitney," allows us a view of both the northeast and southwest sides of the ridge. The sun hits the southwest slope at a high angle all year long and as we would expect, it is drier than the northeast slope and supports smaller, sparser vegetation. The northeast slope receives more shade, retains moisture better, and supports larger plants. Spring wildflowers are found in both climates so look for Chinese Houses,

Everlasting, Deerweed, Wild Cucumber, Yellow Star Thistle, Cliff Aster, and many others.

The trail passes the base of a basalt outcrop, then circles around to the west side before continuing downhill. Look for Spike Moss on the outcrop. As we enter the Southern Oak Woodland, dominated by Coast Live Oaks, look for Goldback ferns, Coastal Wood-fern, Heart-leaved Penstemon, and again, a large colony of Milkwort. The trail ends at the museum. Some log sections nearby will give those with patience a chance to count the rings, to determine the age of the tree.

Coast Live Oak

Distance:	1/2 mile roundtrip
Elevation:	200' gain and loss
Terrain:	Trail and streamside
Trailhead:	Piuma Road

AREA FEATURES

Dark Canyon is the course of an intermittent stream originating high on the western slope of the Saddle Peak ridge. In deep shade at 700' elevation the canyon is a coldwater environment of Riparian Woodland. White Alders and Sycamores dominate.

The trail comes over a ridge, down to the stream, and after crossing climbs the steep western slope of the mountain.

TRAIL INFORMATION

From Malibu Canyon/Las Virgenes Road go east on Piuma Road about 1.3 miles to a U-turn to the right, and park.

We begin the walk by going northeast up a chaparral flanked trail to a ridge. The trail turns right and contours along the hillside before dropping down to the stream crossing.

Big-berry Manzanita

Near the trailhead we will see Yuccas blooming from the first of May for several months, some large Woolly Blue Curls with a long blooming period beginning in March, Big-berry Manzanita, and Chamise. Golden Yarrow, Yellow Star Thistle, Scarlet Larkspur, and Peonies are found in openings of the chaparral.

At the ridge we find some Ceanothus; Buck-brush, Hoary-leaved, and Bigpod, along with Mountain Mahogany, Holly-leaf Cherry, and Holly-leaf Redberry. Look for a few Climbing Penstemons and several scattered Milkworts.

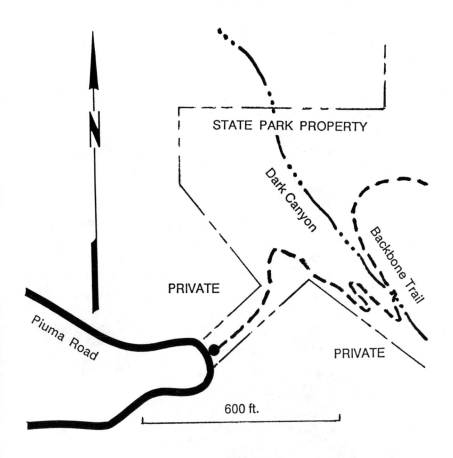

DARK CANYON

Poison Oak, Bay, Flowering Ash, Walnut, Sycamore and White Alder Trees dominate the approach to Dark Canyon. At a switchback near the stream, look for grapes, the main reason for the walk. These natives are all along the stream, and flower and set fruit in May. Of the 700 species of the Grape Family throughout the world, only one is native to our mountains, *Vitis girdiana*; and Dark Canyon is one of the few places where we can find it. The trail crosses the stream and leaves it as the climb up the Saddle Peak ridge begins. We are on a section of the Backbone Trail and may walk for miles if we care to. For today's walk we turnaround at the stream or spend some time walking along its banks. Look for Humboldt Lily, a domestic Geranium, Ferns, and Scarlet Monkey Flower. Shellfish fossils can be found in some of the stream boulders.

White Alder

California
Sycamore

Desert Grape

93

Distance:	2 miles roundtrip
Elevation:	600' gain and loss
Terrain:	Fireroad and trail
Trailhead:	Stunt Road 0.98 miles
	from Mulholland Highway

AREA FEATURES

Near Stunt Road where Cold Creek comes down from the south, massive sandstone mountains rise steeply from the floor of the valley. Our destination today is among these rocky outcrops. Here we will find Santa Susana Tarweed.

TRAIL INFORMATION

From Mulholland Highway drive 1 mile on Stunt Road to a parking lot on the right. A sign reads "Stunt High Trail." We cross Stunt Road, walk a hundred yards downhill and go uphill on Calabasas Peak Motorway (Red Rock Road). During the walk uphill we can see Chaparral on both sides of the fireroad, intermixed with areas of Coastal Sage Scrub. Greenbark Ceanothus, Bigpod Ceanothus, Mountain Mahogany, Toyon, and Laurel Sumac are the largest shrubs; Black Sage, Bush Mallow, Bush Sunflower, California Buckwheat, Deerweed, and Sagebrush are smaller. Sawtooth Goldenbush, Cliff Aster, Wand Chicory, Woolly Aster, Clarkia and a host of spring wildflowers grow on the roadcut and other disturbed places. Red Shank is seen well down the western slope. We may have already noticed the 20' high treelike shrubs with shredding bark, when we drove along Stunt Road.

After 15 minutes of steady walking we reach a saddle and a road division with a choice of continuing ahead toward Calabasas Peak or of walking on the road to the right that drops down Red Rock Canyon. We will stay on the road ahead and in 5 minutes begin looking for Santa Susana Tarweed growing in cracks of sandstone slabs on the right. Tilted sandstone slabs dominate the mountain and are habitat of tarweed. Nearly all of the rocks

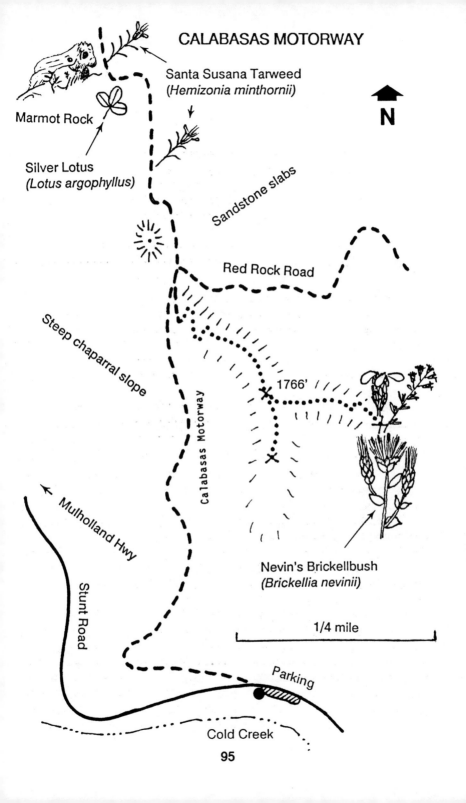

CALABASAS MOTORWAY

N

Santa Susana Tarweed
(*Hemizonia minthornii*)

Marmot Rock

Silver Lotus
(*Lotus argophyllus*)

Sandstone slabs

Red Rock Road

Steep chaparral slope

Calabasas Motorway

1766'

Mulholland Hwy

Stunt Road

Nevin's Brickellbush
(*Brickellia nevinii*)

1/4 mile

Parking

Cold Creek

95

support scattered plants. Marmot Rock, on the left side of the road, is a distinctive landmark and another place to find Tarweed. Silver Lotus and the plentiful Wand Buckwheat share the habitat.

"Marmot Rock" near Calabasas Motorway

After being satisfied that Santa Susana Tarweed grows in solid rock and that it smells like raspberries taste, we can turn around and return downhill. Upon reaching the saddle and a road division we might elect to get up onto the ridge heading south to look for Nevin's Brickelbush.

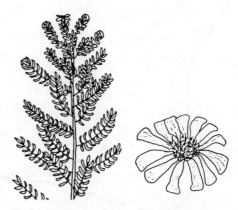

Santa Susana Tarweed

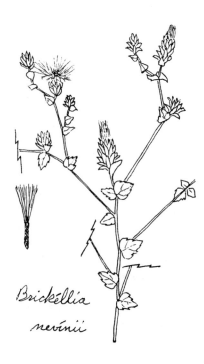

Brickellia
nevinii

Little Brickellbush

An old dirt road takes us to a steep trail along the crest. A slight change in vegetation takes place at the ridge. Bigberry Manzanita, Wand Buckwheat, Hoary Fuchsia, and Woolly Aster are found, and after the third switchback look for Scarlet Bugler. We may want to turn back here because the trail is steep and rocky, calling for mountain climbing footgear, and experience. Perezia, Giant Rye, and Sagebrush dot a small ridge south of Peak 1766. A sharp rocky ridge a couple of hundred yards east can be reached by going cross-country down a steep slope and up to the ridge. Narrow-leaved Milkweed, Lupine, and spring blooming flowers cover the grassy slope. The ridge is our turnaround point. We will explore around the rocks and find Nevin's Brickellbrush before heading back to the trailhead.

Lotus argophyllus

Silver Lotus

Distance:	1½ miles roundtrip
Elevation:	200' gain and loss
Terrain:	Road and trail
Trailhead:	Stunt Road

AREA FEATURES

Each year, right after the winter rains, plants show exceptional growth and we look for the advent of flowers. This event happens throughout the Santa Monicas on hillsides and fields alike, and for some south facing dry inland slopes, the flowering period can be short indeed. Later in the year, when most of the hills are dry, we can make notable discoveries by nosing around in the streams and canyons. Cold Creek is such a place. It flows all year, and has as its source several springs high on the north facing slope of the mountain. A trail goes down Cold Creek. Another trail intersects it and goes uphill through the Stunt Ranch, and farther uphill another trail goes through a magnificent chaparral plant community. The name "Stunt High Trail" is being applied to this trail complex. Our walk today will be only along the stream, so no one should mind if we call it "Cold Creek Trail."

Spring is hard to beat, but we will make this walk at other times to see how the running stream and a protected area extend the season.

TRAIL INFORMATION

The parking lot for the trailhead is I mile east on Stunt Road from Mulholland Hwy. A rack for bicycles is nearby. The trail begins at the east end of the parking area, and after going through a gate heads for the stream.

The parking lot and the part of the trail to Cold Creek offers an opportunity to see many flowers without walking far. The customary Red-stem filaree, Mustard, Bur Clover, Yellow Sweet Clover, Wild Cucumber, and a variety of grasses can be seen from

the car. Before reaching the gate we will see spring blooms of
Blue Dicks, Catalina Mariposa Lily, Sugar Bush, Chamise, and
Golden Yarrow.

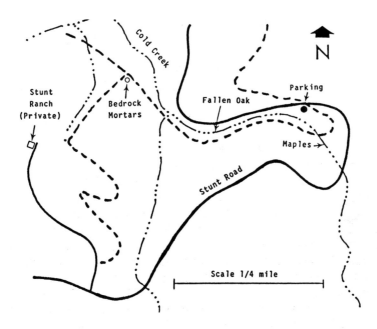

Beyond the gate on the right, near the "No Smoking on Trail"
sign, a Greenbark Ceanothus is somewhat unusual in that most of
the larger leaves are 3-veined rather than 1-veined. The smaller
leaves are 1-veined as we expect.

A Laurel Sumac tree on the left may be covered with an
annual parasitic plant, Dodder. Dodder plants sprout from seeds in
the spring and those plants that are near an acceptable host will
attach and continue to grow. Those that do not find a host plant,
die. Soon after attaching to the host plant, Dodder loses its roots
and lower stem to become completely dependent for all nourishment
on the host plant — in this case Laurel Sumac. Dodder blooms in
the summer, dropping seeds on the ground so that the same process
can begin next year. The orange-yellow, viney stems look as if a
few hundred yards of colored spaghetti are entangled with the
plant. The very small flowers are in dense clusters spaced along
the vine, are white, have a small 5-pointed bell-shaped corolla, and
bloom from June through October. While still in sight of the
parking lot we find Purple Sage, California Sagebrush, Poison Oak,

California Buckwheat, Yucca, Toyon, and Bigpod Ceanothus. In July, only the Buckwheat is still in bloom, the sagebrush blooms later.

The next segment of the trail is bordered by scrub oak on both sides. These small dense tough trees are loaded with acorns in July. The acorns are about 3/4 inch long and still growing. After passing a culvert on the left, we enter the shade of Coast Live Oaks. Coast Live Oaks or "Encina," in Spanish, from which the name of the town of Encino comes, is much larger than Scrub Oak, usually has fewer acorns and has a larger leaf — sometimes 2¼ inches long. The individual leaf is saucer shaped and would float like a little boat if dropped upside down in water. The under side of new leaves has a woolly tuft of hairs at the vein axils — "hairy armpits" if you will. Also, and this takes a l0 power hand lens to see, small fine white starbursts can be found on the surface of the leaf. Both species of oak are found almost side by side here, so we have an opportunity to make a direct comparison for future identification. Oak galls can be seen in this area, mostly on the Scrub Oaks. Golfball sized oak galls are caused by a wasp laying eggs in the base of a leaf. The oak responds by growing a gall, which in turn provides food for the wasp larvae.

The trail continues, taking a right turn on its way to Cold Creek. On the left we notice some beehives in a clearing beyond some oaks. I counted 100 hives and kept my distance. Many chaparral plants are a source of nectar for the bees. Notice the spectacular Poison Oak near the trail as we make a quick transition from Chaparral to Riparian Woodland near the stream. Sycamores line the stream. These large trees with their big soft palmate leaves and light colored exfoliating bark are found in most of the canyons of the Santa Monicas. Flowers are borne in spherical, pendulous heads, the staminate flowers in 3/8 inch diameter balls, the pistillate in 1 inch diameter balls. Both types of flowers grow on each tree. Botanically the fruit is an aggregate of achenes. Flowering occurs February to April and the spherical heads become dry and remain on the tree for several months.

Several beautiful and exceptionally large Coast Live Oaks are near the trail. Spectacular oaks will be a feature of today's walk. A medley of plants awaits us at the stream: Canyon Sunflower, Phacelia, Hairyleaf Ceanothus (which is not always hairy), Watercress, Scarlet Monkey Flower, White Hedge Nettle, Blackberry, Wild Rose, and others. We will take a short sidetrip upstream for about 100 feet to look at a couple of 35 foot high Big Leaf Maple trees. Maples are rare in the Santa Monicas because they need cool running water at their root zone and a protected canyon environment. Here, Maple leaves begin to turn color in July's heat, beginning with the outside edges and working inward until the entire leaf is a yellow-brown. The leaves will drop in the fall, the winged seeds will remain on the tree well into winter.

The trail crosses the stream then angles away from it for a few hundred feet. We look for Wild Rose, Elderberry, Snowberry, Canyon Sunflower, Nightshade, Bush Mallows 12 feet high, and Poison Oak climbing up into the trees. The Poison Oak berries turn from light green to whitish in early summer. Several flowering Ash trees are found in this area, one of which I estimate is 35 feet high. We don't get our hopes up over the name "flowering" because the flowers are not spectacular, having but 2 white petals, each 3/16 of an inch long. Flowering occurs in April to May.

Flowering Ash

200 yards beyond the stream crossing, the trail nears the water again. We will see some Hollyleaf Redberry bushes, Walnut trees that will bear green 1¼ inch ovoid fruit. Another Maple can be seen on the other side of the stream. A Coast Live Oak fell across the stream a few years ago and some of the roots are still in the soil. The tree is alive and growing well. A wood bench allows a sitting down rest stop. It is possible to reach the stream at this point and is well worth it because we are treated to Stream Orchids. Blooming begins late in April for orchids in the Cold

Creek area and by June most of the blossoms have dried and seedpods are forming. Stream Orchids are found in other places but to walk down to the creek to look at a fallen oak and find orchids — that is indeed a pleasant extra surprise. By August, Scarlet Monkey Flowers will be in bloom within sight downstream. We see blackberry vines and momentarily avoid them because of our conditioned response to Poison Oak that also has 3 leaflets.

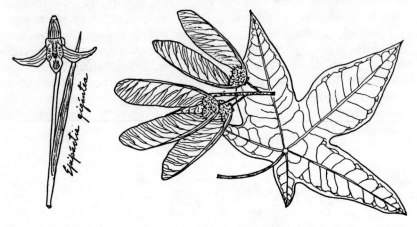

Stream Orchid

Bigleaf Maple

Most of the Ceanothus found on the dry slopes is "Bigpod" with some "Greenbark," but near the stream a few "Hairyleaf" are found. Hairyleaf Ceanothus is rarely found at this low altitude. We normally would need to climb high on the moist, north slopes of Boney Mountain or Saddle Peak. The trail pulls away from the stream for several hundred yards. We can see the canyon below but because of the steep slope and the Poison Oak we will not elect to investigate. The Toyon trees will carry a few white blossoms into early summer, but most petals have fallen and cymes of green berries are forming. Coffeeberry bushes, usually found in the shade, have few green berries. Coffeeberry gets its name because later in the fall the berries ripen and the seeds are sometimes roasted and ground, then used as a coffee substitute. Because Coffeeberries contain glycosides that are laxatives, some care must be taken. We do not pick these berries because the Stunt Ranch property is a park and everything is to be left alone. The rose-purple flowers of Polygala are all but gone in July. Flowering begins early in June and could last into August in a year with good rainfall. Look on the left of the trail for nice stand of these slender shrubs. At one time I believed Polygala to be rare in

Polýgala cornúta
var Fishiae

Milkwort

the Santa Monicas; a few bushes along the stream in Upper Zuma, and a 25 foot diameter group near the stream in Topanga Meadows being the sum total of my knowledge — then one day I noticed the large stand of plants at Cold Creek. Plummer Baccharis grows in the same area and has a similar appearance. Spanish Broom with its yellow pea-like blossoms is scattered farther along the trail. The blooming period starts in March and comes to a close in July when pods have begun to form. Climbing penstemons bloom in May and June — we may see a stray

flower later if we look in deep shade. Cliff Asters bloom most of the year — some are found here. Another ash tree, this one has a trunk almost 15 inches in diameter, grows along the trail. A Hollyleaf Cherry is in its shade.

Several species of ferns are found along the streambed, mostly on the shadier (east facing) slope. We look for Maidenhair Fern, Goldback Fern, Coastal Wood Fern, and Polypody. Farther down the trail we find Mulefat, Bush Monkey Flower, Honeysuckle, Humboldt Lilies, and a hillside of Canyon Sunflowers. The Trail crosses a major intermittent stream coming down the hill from the left, and within 2 minutes we enter an area dominated by chaparral plants. A trail forks to the left — the Stunt High Trail. This is our turnaround point. A large sandstone boulder prominently displays several bedrock mortars, once used by Chumash Indians for acorn grinding.

The trail downstream from this point goes into oak woodlands flanked by chaparral: Mountain Mahogany, Ceanothus, and Redshanks. California Thistle, Yellow Yarrow, Crimson Sage, and other flowering plants grow along the trail and in the open areas.

On the return walk we usually see plants missed on the way in, and plants not listed here will be seen so we keep looking.

Distance:	2 - 4 miles roundtrip
Elevation:	100 - 400' loss and gain
Terrain:	Trail
Trailhead:	Stunt Road

AREA FEATURES

The Saddle Creek watershed offers grasslands, Southern Oak Woodlands, Riparian Woodlands, and a lot of Chaparral. A fire in 1970 burned much of the area and recovery is complete. The plant communities have maintained their native integrity in most of the area with some major exceptions in the grasslands that have been used for grazing. There, Mustard, Filaree, and many grasses have become established.

The Saddle Creek Trail, built in 1987, is a segment of the Backbone Trail. Today's walk will be on the upper part between 1700 and 2000 feet of elevation on the north slope of Saddle Peak. Of special interest is the Chaparral. Some 10' high *Pickeringia montana* bushes are found on at least one ridge, and I suspect that with some independent exploration you would find more. *Ceanothus cuneatus* is another special feature of the walk. I do not know of another area where this Buckbrush is as available. *Ceanothus oliganthus, C. spinosus,* and *C. megacarpus* are all plentiful. Chaparral restricts the plant species that are allowed in the community but this Chaparral has open spaces, grasslands, and streambeds so that Ferns, Fuchsias, Prickly Phlox, Crimson Sage, Mariposa Lilies and many other "flowers" are found.

TRAIL INFORMATION

From Mulholland Highway drive 2.8 miles on Stunt Road and park off the road about 200 yards uphill from the Saddle Creek Ranch entrance. An old road leaves Stunt Road on the south side and initially heads west but turns south almost immediately. At this point we leave the road to continue west on a trail going along a grassland, then slightly uphill until entering an Oak Woodland.

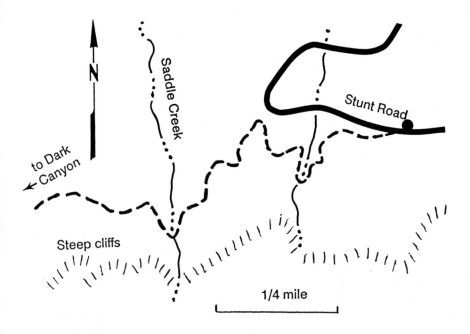

During the first quarter mile look for Eastwood Manzanita, Golden Yarrow, Deerweed, California Everlasting (smells like maple sugar), Coyote Brush, Bush Lupine, and upon nearing the Oak Woodland — Poison Oak. Several very large, robust, fifteen-foot-high bushes are along the fringe of the wooded area.

The trail goes under the shade of Coast Live Oaks, beside some large sandstone boulders, crosses a creekbed and makes a right turn. Look for several tree-like Hairy-leaf Ceanothus bushes. In early March their deep blue flowers make this a special place. In about 200 yards we come to another streambed and Bay Trees! Then a leaning Coast Live Oak causes the trail to make a jog to the right. Time yourself from the leaning oak and in one minute begin to look for Chaparral Pea bushes along a ridge. *Pickeringia montana* comes into bloom in late April or early May, giving a deep pink tint to the Chaparral. Seldom found in the Santa Monicas and always a delight when in bloom, the Chaparral Pea is a pleasant ten minute walk from the trailhead.

Two minutes later along the trail a large sandstone outcrop on the left marks the area of the Buck-brush Ceanothus. The white blossoms appear in January and the triangular seedpods are well-formed by April. We are given a good chance to compare Buck-brush and Big-pod Ceanothus. both have thick, corky stipules at the base of the leaf stalk; both have small, leather-like leaves but slightly differing in shape; both are 10-12' shrubby evergreen plants. The Buck-brush has opposite leaves, opposite spur branchlets, and small triangular seedpods. The Big-pod has alternate leaves and large somewhat globular seedpods. About ten minutes after going through the Buck-brush area the trail crosses a ridge and enters a substantial forest of Big-pod Ceanothus on a west facing slope.

After crossing a level meadow the trail continues west and drops down toward a prominent streambed. Enroute, we go through a sizeable area of 15' high Bush Mallow. Look for flowers from April into summer. For the purpose of this walk we have reached a turnaround point, but first look downstream on the right side to see a half dozen Fremont Cottonwood trees. The trail continues two more miles and a 1000' elevation loss to Dark Canyon and a trailhead on Piuma Road. Another walk will take us to Dark Canyon.

A brisk walking pace without stopping to look at anything would get us in and out in 1 hour and 15 minutes. Plan to take 2½ hours because you will find little canyons to explore and many plants to identify.

Pickeringia montana

Chaparral Pea

This walk features chaparral plants, and because the 6 species of Ceanothus that grow in the Santa Monica Mountains constitute an important segment of the chaparral plant community, I've added a keying chart for Ceanothus. This chart is supposed to help identify each of the six species at any time of year.

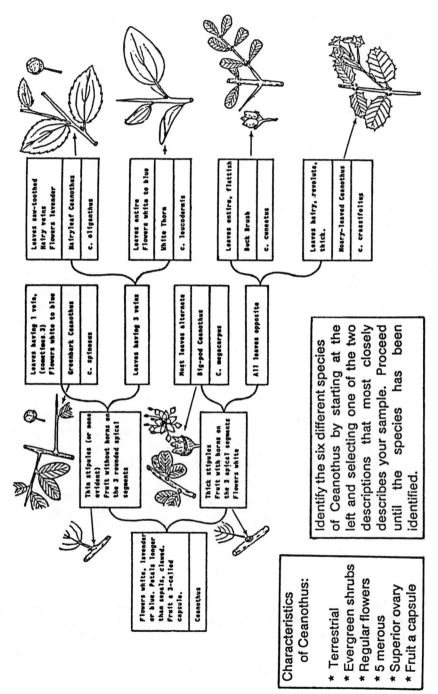

Hairyleaf Ceanothus
c. oliganthus

Leaves saw-toothed
Hairy veins
Flowers lavender

White Thorn
c. leucodermis

Leaves entire
Flowers white to blue

Buck Brush
c. cuneatus

Leaves entire, flattish

Hoary-leaved Ceanothus
c. crassifolius

Leaves hairy, revolute, thick.

Greenbark Ceanothus
c. spinosus

Leaves having 1 vein, (sometimes 3)
Flowers white to blue

Leaves having 3 veins

Big-pod Ceanothus
c. megacarpus

Most leaves alternate

All leaves opposite

Thin stipules (or none evident)
Fruit without horns on the 3 rounded apical segments

Thick stipules
Fruit with horns on the 3 apical segments
Flowers white

Ceanothus

Flowers white, lavender or blue. Petals longer than sepals, clawed. Fruit a 3-celled capsule.

Identify the six different species of Ceanothus by starting at the left and selecting one of the two descriptions that most closely describes your sample. Proceed until the species has been identified.

Characteristics
of Ceanothus:

* Terrestrial
* Evergreen shrubs
* Regular flowers
* 5 merous
* Superior ovary
* Fruit a capsule

Distance:	4 miles (2 miles if a car shuttle is used)
Elevation:	900' gain and loss
Terrain:	Trail
Trailhead:	Stunt Road

AREA FEATURES

In prehistoric times Cold Creek Canyon was occupied by Native American Indians — the Chumash or their predecessors. The year-round stream and ready access to food made the canyon an attractive place in which to live. During the Spanish and Mexican occupations, land grants, in common with much of the Malibu Creek watershed, were not awarded in Cold Creek. Homesteading of government land was encouraged by the United States but it wasn't until the turn of the century that a German immigrant named Herman Hethke settled in upper Cold Creek. He filed for the Homestead in 1909. The Murphys bought the property in 1919 and after Mrs. Murphy's death in 1927, her daughter Kathleen took charge of the property. Fire destroyed the house in 1936 and a new ranch house was built and lasted 34 years until the fire of 1970 swept through the area. Kathleen gave the property to the Nature Conservancy in 1970 as a preserve, in honor of her mother "Ida Haines Murphy." The lower 80 acres, which includes the lower gate, was sold to the Nature Conservancy in 1976 by Alfred Perrson. In 1984 the Nature Conservancy transferred ownership of the Preserve to the Mountains Restoration Trust.

The Preserve is 565 acres of wild land, most of it on steep slopes. It supports diverse communities of plant and animal life. The Trust has continued the policy of the Nature Conservancy and has set aside the Preserve as a sanctuary for educational and scientific uses. Those of us who would like to visit the preserve may do so on a permit basis by contacting the Mountains Restoration Trust in Malibu, several days in advance of our intended visit.

MURPHY PRESERVE
(UPPER COLD CREEK TRAIL)

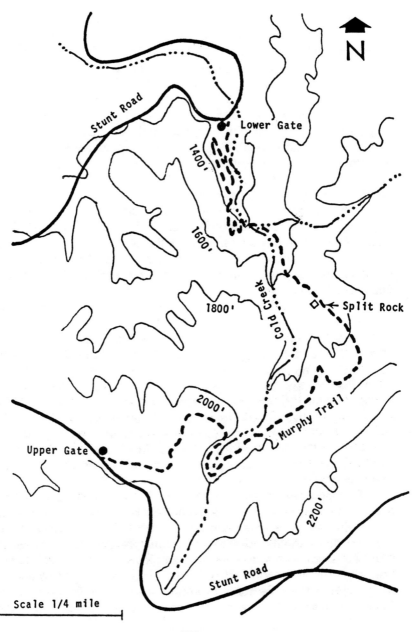

N

Stunt Road

1400'

Lower Gate

1600'

Cold Creek

1800'

◇ ← Split Rock

2000'

Murphy Trail

Upper Gate

2200'

Stunt Road

Scale 1/4 mile

TRAIL INFORMATION

Permit required.

Park off Stunt Road 3.4 miles from its intersection with Mulholland Highway. The upper entrance is through a gate in the fence. If our plan is to car shuttle we will need another car at the lower gate. We also need the combination to the lock at the lower gate.

We follow the old "Murphy driveway" from the upper gate. It drops us down on a gentle grade through a canopy of Red-shanks and other chaparral plants. A feeling of expectancy to Cold Creek mounts from the moment we enter the canopy of trees over the trail, and the feeling grows as each new turn in the trail develops. When we reach a wooden shelter look for handout literature and check the bulletin board. Several sandstone boulders with marine shell fossils are displayed here. Pectin (Vertipectin nevadanus) lived in the ocean when this area was below the sea.

Our trail continues through chaparral with an occasional dip into oak woodlands. On this north and east facing slope the chaparral is high so as to often form a canopy over the trail, belying the adage that chaparral is "too low to give shade." Scrub Oak is plentiful; watch for the rarer interior Live Oak. The trail enters an area of lower vegetation; many of the plants are Chamise. Chamise sprouts from the roots after a fire and is quick to generate itself so has made a successful recovery in Cold Creek after the 1970 fire burned the chaparral to the ground. After Chamise reaches an age of 15 years it seems to slow its growth. This is done in part by the drying of some branch tips. I have heard people speak out in alarm about the "Chaparral dying" when this normal condition is observed. We can make our own observations here because the 1970 fire gives us an accurate date from which to measure growth.

Farther down the trail Ceanothus begins to make up a good part of the chaparral. Bigpod Ceanothus is dominant here; we also easily find Hairyleaf Ceanothus and White Thorn. Three other species of Ceanothus are found in the preserve, but not readily. The trail becomes sandy underfoot and levels out for a short length. We will find several Manzanita bushes on our right. The smooth red stems sprout from the roots of shrubs that burned in the 1970 fire. Eastwood Manzanita root crown sprouts, Bigberry Manzanita does not. We will see some Bigberry Manzanitas farther along the trail — it only grows from seed and lacks a burl.

Farther down the trail we periodically walk through Coastal Sage Scrub plant communities. A prominent plant is California Buckwheat *(Eriogonum fasciculatum).* From the Latin, fascicle means "little bundle," descriptive of the clusters of needle-like leaves. California Buckwheat blooms heavily during spring and summer and to a lesser degree throughout the year. Bees from hives downstream of the preserve gather "Buckwheat honey" from these plants. At the overlook point Cold Creek Canyon is more than tree deep. We look across to see Chalk Dudleya plants on the rocky slopes, and down to see a few Bigleaf Maples crowded in with the oaks. Farther, as the trail winds down to the stream, we will find a Maple close to us.

The trail enters an Oak Woodland and soon we see a rusty pick-up truck. During the 1970 fire the truck was used to haul furniture from the house; the flames came up the hill so the driver got out and ran, but the truck and house burned.

Next is one of the most impressive stands of Poison Oak around; on both sides of the trail and head high in places. Notice the California Blackberry mixed in to deceive the unwary. Below the Poison Oak area we see a marsh on the right. The sandstone hillside soaks up the winter rains, and years later, after filtering through many layers of rock, the water surfaces. We are near a major seepage that remains damp even during the driest periods. Kathleen Murphy planted the yellow iris which has naturalized in the marshy area and below. The iris begins flowering in April. Bracken ferns are found along the marsh and on damp slopes. Some Giant Chain ferns can be seen on the far side of the marsh. Humboldt Lilies are found in the marsh area and along the stream to the lowest part of the Preserve.

Immediately below the marsh we find a clear spring that was used as a water supply by Herman Hethke. Hethke notched the inside of the nearby split sandstone boulder and placed rafters, then covered the "house" with corrugated sheet steel. This qualified as a house under the Homestead law and Herman Hethke became the owner of a 160-acre ranch.

The trail below the boulder house is steep. Periodically a part of the lower trail is wiped out by landslide. In 1985 repairs were made to a section that had become impassable and for the time being is usable. If you aren't prepared for the steep trail it would be advisable to return the way you came. The steep north facing slope of the mountain is well shaded and supports the growth of Bay trees, Snowberry, Crimson Pitcher Sage, Woodferns and other shade loving plants. Down in the canyon on our left we are able to pick out some Bigleaf Maple trees. The 26 or so maples here constitute a relict plant community that has lived in this cool-damp canyon since pre-pleistocene times.

After another steep section of trail we cross a small wooden foot bridge. Giant Horsetails are found in the stream on the left; a small waterfall comes over a notch in a massive sandstone ledge on the right. Calcium carbonate deposits drape down the face of the waterfall, and Venus-hair Fern (Adiantum capillis-veneris) grows on the sandstone. This fern requires some calcium for growth and is nearly always found on moist rock. Maiden-hair Fern (Adiantum jordanii) is usually found in moist shady places, but growing in soil.

The trail eases up a bit, then continues downhill and crosses the creek. At one point the trail switchbacks uphill so as to avoid a steep area of the hillside. Soon after, we pass a large field of Bracken Fern on our right. Some steep places are ahead but, shortly we come to a fork in the trail and turn right.

We follow the trail upstream and at the stream crossing will notice the first of many Stream Orchids. April and May are the best time to see the blooms. The grasslike shoots grow from cracks in rocks, first becoming noticeable in February. If for no other reason, one should take this walk to see the orchids. Look for some Leather Root shrubs along the stream. A small waterfall is our turnaround point. The pool at the base is likely to have a newt or two during spring, then they migrate from the water to damp places under leaves, rocks or logs. More orchids grow in the waterfall area. We also will note the large slab of calcium carbonate draping down the face of the falls.

Our use permit does not include the area along the creek above the falls; there is no trail and travel could seriously damage the fragile plant life. We return by going back down the trail to the lower gate. The gate is kept locked so when we request a use permit, it is important to make arrangements to have the gate unlocked. A car shuttle makes the return trip convenient but by using Stunt Road and the Stunt High Trail we can get a pleasant extra 2 miles of walking.

Venus Maidenhair Fern

AREA FEATURES

This part of Cold Creek is in a deep shady canyon. Water flows throughout the year making this a true riparian woodland. The land belongs to The Mountains Restoration Trust, obtained from the Nature Conservancy in 1984. The Nature Conservancy had bought the lower canyon from Alfred Perrson in 1976.

Visiting the preserve is by permit which may be obtained from The Mountains Restoration Trust in Malibu. Because of use for educational purposes, and a limit in the number that can enter the area, any request should be made in advance. The Trust is a non-profit organization and depends upon contributions for support, and although there is no charge for entry, a donation helps maintain this valuable resource.

TRAIL INFORMATION

PERMIT REQUIRED.

Park off Stunt Road about 1.3 miles from its intersection with Mulholland Highway. Two areas across the road from the preserve will hold a dozen cars. When you apply for a permit from The Mountains Restoration Trust, arrangements will be made to unlock the gate. An almost level trail follows the west bank of the trail passing Wild Cucumber, Phacelia, Peony, Crimson Pitcher Sage, Cliff Aster and Purple Nightshade. Greenbark Ceanothus and Hairy-leaved Ceanothus bracket the trail. In 100 yards we enter a wooded area shaded by Coast Live Oaks. Miner's Lettuce, Milkmaids, and Canyon Sunflower are found in the filtered sunshine. We will take the trail in a counter clockwise loop so we pass by the trail coming up from the stream at a 90° angle and continue ahead. Soon, a trail branches right and switches back uphill. We will go straight ahead slightly downhill and along the stream, passing some Bay trees, Giant Rye, Bracken Fern, Blackberry vines and Humboldt Lilies. At the stream crossing look for Leather Root, Celery, Watercress, Willow, and Stream Orchids. The trail soon turns to walking on streambed rocks. An eight-foot waterfall in two steps is our turnaround point. The area beyond has been set aside as a preserve because of its fragile nature. We are not allowed beyond the waterfall. Notice the stalagmite-like shape at the face of the waterfalls. Precipitation of calcium carbonate from the water has built drape-like aprons reaching the lower pool, and part way down to the upper pool. Look for Venus Maidenhair Fern, Polypody Fern, Stream Orchids, California Fuchsia, and Rose bushes near the stream.

On the way back downstream a steep trail goes uphill on our right. This will complete the loop by taking us up the hill and back down to the stream at the oak woodland near the entrance gate. The map indicates some of the plants found. After crossing the stream we go up to the trail we came on and then to the gate.

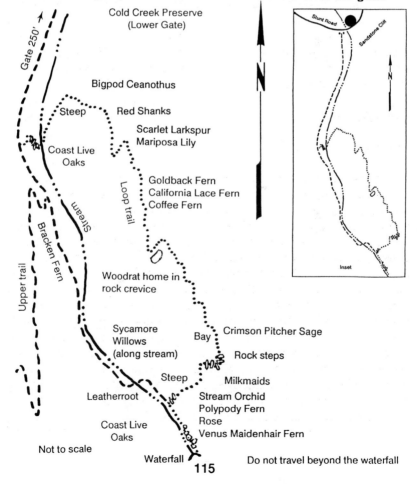

Cold Creek Preserve
(Lower Gate)

Gate 250'

Bigpod Ceanothus

Steep   Red Shanks

Scarlet Larkspur
Mariposa Lily

Coast Live
Oaks

Goldback Fern
California Lace Fern
Coffee Fern

Loop trail

Stream

Bracken Fern

Upper trail

Woodrat home in
rock crevice

Sycamore
Willows   Bay   Crimson Pitcher Sage
(along stream)

Rock steps

Steep   Milkmaids

Leatherroot

Stream Orchid
Polypody Fern
Rose
Venus Maidenhair Fern

Coast Live
Oaks

Not to scale

Waterfall   Do not travel beyond the waterfall

Stunt Road   Sandstone Cliff

N

Inset

115

Distance:	3 miles roundtrip
Elevation:	700' gain and loss
Terrain:	Trail
Trailhead:	Mulholland Highway

AREA FEATURES

Built in 1985 by volunteers, this trail is an easement across private land given by the owner for public use.

Chaparral is the primary plant community, mixed with areas of Coastal Sage Scrub. A few Grasslands, Southern Oak Woodlands and Cliffsides are also found.

TRAIL INFORMATION

Drive 1.9 miles west of Old Topanga Road on Mulholland Highway. Park on the east side of the road in the vicinity of roadmarker 27.15. Because of activities associated with development, part of the trail has disappeared so we must look around for its beginning. The trail is easy to follow once we find the trailhead.

The plants found here are somewhat common, but 3 reasons accumulatively make the area interesting: (1) Its easy access from the west end of the San Fernando Valley; (2) We will see the largest Holly-leaf Cherry found locally; and (3) An extensive display of Spike Moss demonstrates that plants select the soil on which they will grow.

The west facing slope at the trail's beginning supports plants that survive a hot dry environment. Look for Deerweed, California Buckwheat, Cliff Aster, and Goldenbush. We will drop down through Coast Live Oaks to an arroyo filled with Snowberry and some Poison Oak. Less than 10 minutes after leaving Mulholland we will make a left turn and leave the sight and sound of the highway. Almost immediately Spike Moss growing on volcanic rock becomes the center of interest. Although common in the Santa Monica Mountains, *Selaginella biglovii* is the only local species of a world-wide distribution of 700 different Spike Mosses. We will notice a distinct relationship between Selaginella and its growth on volcanic rock, on this trail and also elsewhere in the Santa Monicas. White Sage in

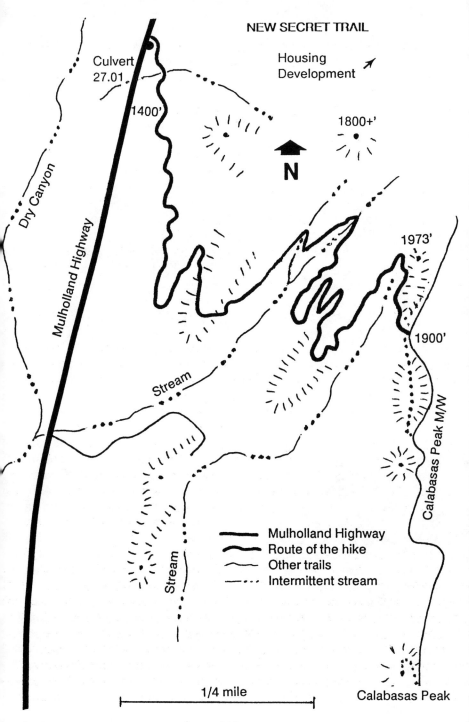

NEW SECRET TRAIL

Culvert
27.01

1400'

Housing
Development

1800+'

Dry Canyon

Mulholland Highway

N

1973'

1900'

Stream

Calabasas Peak M/W

Stream

━━━━ Mulholland Highway
━━━━ Route of the hike
─── Other trails
·-·-· Intermittent stream

1/4 mile

Calabasas Peak

scattered plants is found along this section of trail. At the base of a west-facing sandstone slope we travel through a well-developed stand of Scrub Oak. Look for golf ball to tennis ball sized galls on some of the leaves.

Scrub Oak

Holly-leaf Cherry

As the trail crosses a broad sandstone ridge and makes a left switchback, it enters a sloping meadow dotted with Coastal Sage Scrub plants. After turning right and crossing a small arroyo look at the shell fossils lying along the trail. These have eroded from the sandstone formation that dominates the area.

We soon begin a serious uphill section of the trail and make some switchbacks. On one stretch of trail after making a sharp left turn, look left for a large Holly-leaf Cherry tree. Several large trunks sprouting from a root crown form a tree having a 30' spread and about 25' high. (If we miss seeing this on the way up, time the return trip — it should take 7 minutes from the turnaround point to the Cherry tree).

We continue uphill to reach Calabasas Motorway, then turn around and return. If we were to go south on Calabasas M/W well beyond the peak, we would find Santa Susana Tarweed and Silver Lotus. This is featured in Walk #17, "Calabasas Motorway."

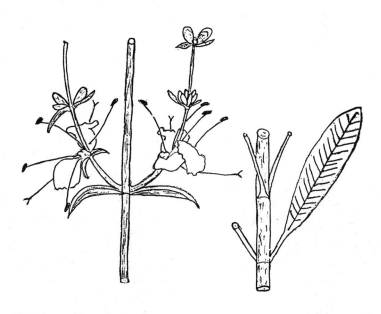

White Sage

Distance:	3 miles
Elevation:	350' gain and loss
Terrain:	Fireroad
Trailhead:	Saddle Peak Road and Stunt Road

AREA FEATURES

Topanga Ridge divides the Malibu and Topanga watersheds. Today's walk will be at the 2400 foot level, at first below the ridge, then along it to a high point where a lookout tower stood for many years before it was removed in the 1970s. The site is owned by the Mountains Restoration Trust and the access road is privately owned. Primarily a Chaparral plant community, the ridge does support some Coastal Sage Scrub plants. A fire swept uphill in 1970 and left only the burned trunks of bushes and trees. Recovery has been complete with only a few burned stumps still visible.

TRAIL INFORMATION

Park off the road at the junction of Stunt Road and Saddle Peak road at the crest of the mountains. The trail is a fireroad leading to the site of the fire lookout. The road is paved for about 500 yards at which point it forks, with the right fork going uphill to a telephone relay tower.

Because the road is paved part way and the grade is reasonably gentle, this wildflower walk can be used by those in wheelchairs. When the pavement ends the road becomes rough but it is hard ground and rock, but passable. Parents with children in strollers might have a problem because the wheels are small.

The first part of the walk is high on the north facing slope of the mountain and although classified as chaparral, the vegetation includes Bay Trees, Coast Live Oaks, Canyon Sunflower, Heart-leaved Penstemon, and some Grassland plants. Toyon with red berries from November until late winter, Scrub Oak with small but many acorns, Russian Thistles and other small shrubs dominate the first part of the walk. Look for Giant Rye, Hairyleaf Ceanothus, Saw-toothed Goldenbush, bush Lupine, Phacelia, Cliff Aster, and Honeysuckle.

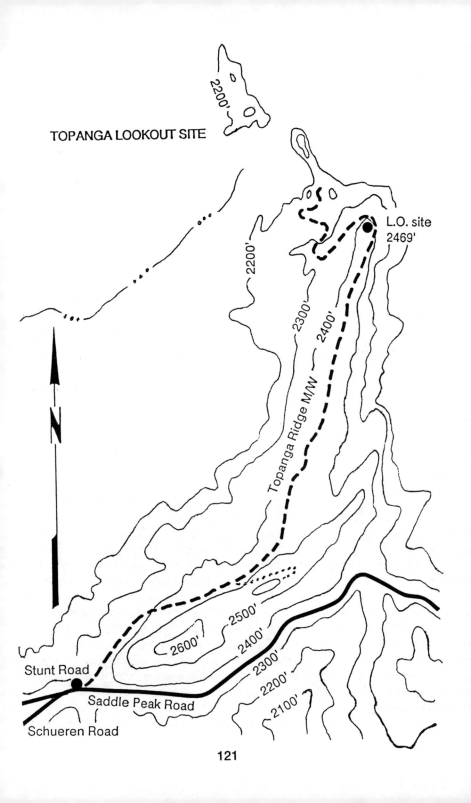

TOPANGA LOOKOUT SITE

2200'

2200'

L.O. site
2469'

Topanga Ridge M/W

2300'

2400'

N

2500'

2600'

2400'

2300'

Stunt Road

Saddle Peak Road

2200'

2100'

Schueren Road

When the trail forks, we go straight ahead onto a hard dirt road.

Geologically most of the rock along the route is sandstone and pebble cobble conglomerate. We will see some immense slabs, usually sloping steeply toward the northwest. Several intrusive sills and dikes of volcanic diabase in the form of weathered spheroidal blocks will be seen in the road and in roadcuts. This volcanic diabase is called "Onion Rock" because it exfoliates as it weathers. Some of this will be found in a roadcut after the route reaches a saddle and makes a definite turn toward north. Wand Buckwheat is the dominant plant on the face of the roadcut.

Wand Buckwheat

Toyon

Later we will cross an area where the pavement of the road shows the distinctive diabase pattern and we have an opportunity to see it up close as we walk.

California Buckwheat, Chaparral Current, Bush Senecio, Big-berry Manzanita, Two-tone Everlasting, Telegraph Weed, and Laurel Sumac will be seen all along this stretch of the road. The lookout site is surrounded by alien Pine Trees. These rarely reproduce in the Santa Monica Mountains, but once established, some species are able to live many years. The lookout site isn't the neatest spot in the mountains. The broken bottle evidence indicates that the spot has been popular as a rendezvous for beer drinkers and careless picnickers.

The road continues around the eastern side of the old lookout, dropping rather steeply. Look for more diabase "Onion Rock" in the roadcut. Bush Poppy, Hollyleaf Cherry, Red Shanks, Hairy-leaved Ceanothus, and Mountain Mahogany are found on the north facing slope alongside the road. Plummer's Baccharis is found in the saddle where we can look into Old Topanga Canyon watershed. The road ends at a sandstone knoll and we can look back to see the large tilted sandstone slabs. A rock scramble trail goes down the ridge northwest from the end of the road, but we won't hike the ridge on this walk and will turnaround to return the way we came. Walk #17 describes the plants at the other end of the ridge.

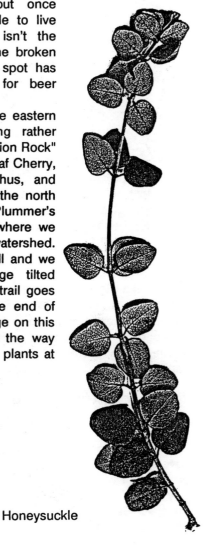

Honeysuckle

123

Distance: 2 miles
Elevation: 400 feet gain and loss
Terrain: Trail
Trailhead: Stunt Road

AREA FEATURES

This segment of trail is from the upper part of the Stunt Ranch into and through the west part of Cold Creek Preserve. Stunt Ranch is owned by the Santa Monica Mountains Conservancy, a state agency that acquires parklands for public use. Cold Creek Preserve was transferred to the Nature Conservancy by Kathleen Murphy about 1970, and the Nature Conservancy gave the land to the Mountains Restoration Trust, a non-profit corporation primarily funded by the Santa Monica Mountains Conservancy.

Most of the trail is in a chaparral plant community having a good mix of plant species worthy of our interest. The Wright Fire of September 1970 thoroughly burned the area of the walk. Some of the burned hardwood trunks of Manzanita and other chaparral plants can still be seen and are markers to show how sprouting from burned root crowns regenerated the chaparral forest.

This walk is on a trail through a pristine area so we will not see any restrooms, drinking fountains, or other conveniences. An immediate sense of being isolated comes over us the moment the trailhead is out of sight and most of us appreciate the chance of getting away from it all and are willing to sacrifice the conveniences.

TRAIL INFORMATION

From Mulholland Highway, drive 1.9 miles on Stunt Road to the Stunt Ranch parking lot. The trail begins across the road and several hundred feet west near mileage marker 1.92. Upon starting up the trail we find ourselves in the shade of Coast Live Oaks and Bay Trees. Coastal Woodfern, Phacelia and Canyon Sunflower line the trail. Beyond the second switchback we leave the filtered shade of the woodland and enter a chaparral forest in which we will continue the rest of the walk. A mixture of plants will be seen

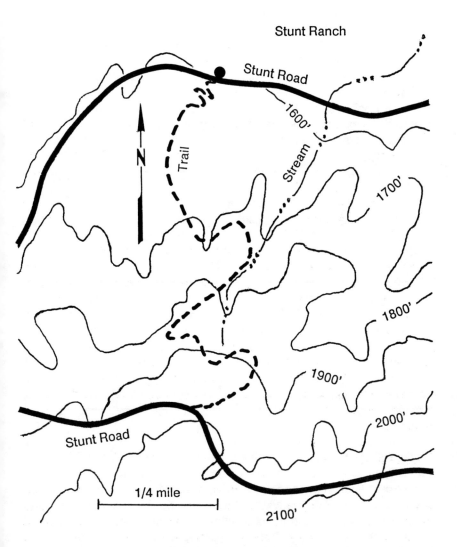

Stunt Ranch

Stunt Road

1600'

Trail

Stream

1700'

N

1800'

1900'

2000'

Stunt Road

2100'

1/4 mile

STUNT HIGH TRAIL

throughout but Manzanita with its reddish bark gains attention immediately. Two species of Manzanita grow in this area; Eastwood Manzanita is the more plentiful — it sprouts from the root crown after a fire, usually in multiple stems. Bigberry Manzanita grows only from seed so will have one stem — still a shrub but grows larger and is more treelike than Eastwood. Chamise and Red Shank are both a part of this chaparral forest. These members of the rose family have needle-like leaves, clustered in Chamise, alternate and single in Red Shank. Red Shank is much larger than Chamise and has a bark that continuously is shredding, giving it another common name, Ribbon Bush. Four species of Ceanothus are found: Buck-brush, Greenstem, Hairyleaf and Bigpod. This chart will allow a quick identification but is only valid in this area.

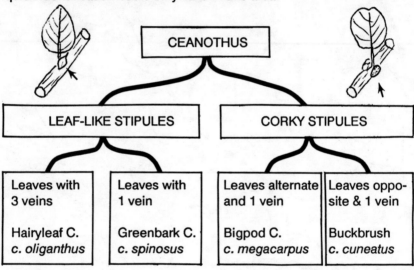

CEANOTHUS			
LEAF-LIKE STIPULES		**CORKY STIPULES**	
Leaves with 3 veins Hairyleaf C. *c. oliganthus*	Leaves with 1 vein Greenbark C. *c. spinosus*	Leaves alternate and 1 vein Bigpod C. *c. megacarpus*	Leaves oppo-site & 1 vein Buckbrush *c. cuneatus*

Buckbrush is by far the dominant Ceanothus along Stunt High Trail and without close observation may be identified as Bigpod.

Scrub Oak, Toyon, Sugar Bush, and farther up the trail, Moun-tain Mahogany and Hollyleaf Redberry add to the larger shrubs composing the chaparral community. The smaller shrubs include Bush Monkey Flower, Yellow Yarrow, Deerweed, Black Sage, Honeysuckle, California Buckwheat, and Heart-leaved Penstemon. Most of the openings along the trail allow the smaller shrubs a foothold and also an opportunity for some herbaceous plants. Silk-tassel bushes are found in at least two areas, and at one place about ten minutes from the upper end of the trail both Manzanita species, several Silk-tassel Bushes, a Sugar Bush, Hairyleaf Ceanothus, Hollyleaf Redberry, and a Greenbark Ceanothus are all found together in a 20-foot stretch along the trail.

The upper end of Stunt High Trail meets Stunt Road near a road sign at mile 2.89. Downroad about 100 yards and on the south side, we will find the trailhead for Saddle Creek Trail (see Walk #19 page 104).

We turn around and walk back still hunting for those elusive Silk-tassel Bushes.

 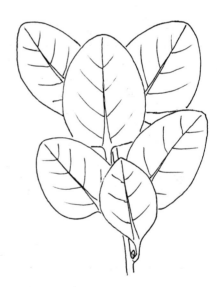

Eastwood Manzanita   Big-berry Manzanita